Runaway Train

The story of a lapsed Salvation Army girl who found true love with an alcoholic street kid

Runaway Train: The story of a lapsed Salvation Army girl who found true love with an alcoholic street kid

This is a work of nonfiction, though names have been changed in places to protect the privacy of some individuals.

ISBN: 978-1-7782332-0-3 (paperback)
ISBN: 978-1-7782332-1-0 (ebook)

Cover Design and Formatting: Krista Cambers

Runaway Train

The story of a lapsed Salvation Army girl who found true love with an alcoholic street kid

Krista Cambers

DEDICATION

This book is dedicated to the love of my life, Mark Cambers, as well as to any who have suffered from addiction, disease, or homelessness at any point in their lives. You are loved more than you may ever know.

PREFACE

When I first met Mark, I never would have dreamed I'd eventually be writing our story. I'd been trying to write a book for years, and nothing had ever come of it. When I first conceived of writing this, I had initially written it for a website. I received some great reactions, with many suggesting I go through with publishing it. There was an outcry of support for the content. I won't lie; it made me emotional. People wrote me about their personal stories of battling addiction or losing someone to alcoholic liver cirrhosis. There were truly more people than I had anticipated who responded. I wanted to share our story because it's common for certain groups of people to be dehumanized by our society, and I wanted to give a voice to the reality of what some are going through.

I'm sometimes met with questions like "Why did you waste your time on him?" or "I'm sure he had plenty of opportunities to change before it got to the point that it did." That's true in a sense. But I find many often overlook all the little nuances of how people get led down the paths that they've been on. Often mental health issues are involved at the core of addiction. In Mark's case, he felt unloved (and that he was a lost cause), and he was depressed. He'd resigned himself for a long time to dying alone. He didn't see much purpose and had even attempted suicide in the past. A lot of the issues behind addiction are swept under the rug. For some, it's easier and more convenient to write it off as people acting "stupid" or "irresponsible" when it goes much deeper.

My goal is to help remove the stigma, help raise awareness of the need for better help for addicts, and reform healthcare relating to diseases caused by addiction and mental health.

Alcohol abuse is so normalized worldwide that if you pay attention while watching a television show or movie, it doesn't take long before you see jokes about it. In many sitcoms, a character will wake up hungover and cannot remember the night before, either embarrassing themselves or sleeping with someone they didn't know or didn't mean to. Becoming blackout drunk is not normal, not healthy, and most of all, in the end, you realize it is not funny. It has natural consequences. In today's world, we normalize what is essentially an overdose.

In the real world, these situations can lead not only to general risky behaviours that could have disastrous effects on our lives but, in the long run, to severe terminal illness. Someone may laugh at the sitcom but turn their nose up at an alcoholic who is panhandling. They need compassion and love...not judgments like saying they should have handled it "some other way." Some people don't know what else to do once they're in so deep, or they've tried other things that didn't work. There are so many reasons and ways to become an addict...please remember that. Mark, was one such person. Please keep an open mind and try to understand how people end up in positions as he did, and how it affected me and the others that loved him throughout his life. Addicts are people who fall in love and have friendships and family just like the rest of us. As I learned through him and the people I met because of him, we all have a story. I remember everything pretty well because every moment with him was special.

I also want to add there's subject matter and language that I originally toned down on the website for those sensitive to it. As a book, I've decided to leave it, as any cursing is simply part of the story and the truth of how things were spoken or went down. I don't want to sugar-coat or change what was said or done, as this is a true story. I have changed the names of most, outside of the four of us who stayed in my house. I did this for privacy reasons as I did not know if they'd want their real names to be used. Some have given me express permission, so there are real names here and there. In any segments of Mark's writing, I've done the same thing. I've also had to edit a bit for grammar, but his work remains intact. I'll introduce Mark and me individually, so you understand where we both come from, and then I'll get into the bulk of our story. These are the last months of the life of someone who was not "just an addict." He loved me very much and will be *forever* loved by me. If true love is a thing...this was it for me.

Krista Cambers
October 2022

"Then the righteous will answer him, saying, 'Lord, when did we see you hungry and feed you, or thirsty and give you a drink? When did we see you as a stranger and take you in, or naked and clothe you? When did we see you sick or in prison and come to you?'

The King will answer them, 'Most certainly I tell you, because you did it to one of the least of these my brothers, you did it to me.'" *from Matthew 25:37-40 (WEB)*

TABLE OF CONTENTS

I SETTING THE STAGE

Who am I? It took me a long time to find the answer to that question; and, of course, I'm still learning. I was born in St. John's, Newfoundland, in the winter of 1983. My mom said when I popped out, I barely made a sound and looked around wide-eyed at the room (though I'm sure I couldn't see anything yet).

I've been looking around at the world and asking myself what is up with this crazy planet ever since.

My family were a part of the Salvation Army and I was introduced to it starting with my dedication as a baby. I grew up with divorced parents (not as common here in this province in the eighties) and lived with my mother and grandparents. My family had a rich background in the denomination, with my grandfather's two younger brothers even in high-ranking positions of Colonel and Lieutenant-colonel within the Salvation Army (Canada and Bermuda Territory).

I've seen an increase over the years of many people who dislike their upbringing in the church (by this, I don't mean the Salvation Army but the general worldwide Christian faith). While my mother often fought with me to get me up on Sunday mornings, I typically enjoyed it once I was there. My childhood church memories are nothing near traumatizing. It was pretty fun. I was lucky compared to some in the various churches out there. It seems everywhere I look, there are people with a lot of childhood church trauma. I especially loved Vacation Bible School one year with the theme "Sonseeker Safari."

Get it? I love a good pun!

As a teen, I drifted away from church. However, a school friend of mine had introduced me to her youth group, which I went to every Friday night. Make no mistake, just because I enjoyed the Bible doesn't mean I behaved myself. I was not always the most well-behaved child, but I meant well. A few times, I'd left youth group to go make out with a guy I was seeing casually. I don't think my school friend ever knew the details of what I did when I left. I'm also not excusing it, just being honest. Teenagers!

I was known for yelling and slamming doors if Mom and I got into it. Things often were not pretty between us, and at times were even ugly. I suffered from being bullied at school relentlessly and wondered why it seemed like my dad's side of the family didn't want me. My self-esteem was terrible. I had horrible acne as a teenager for a couple of years and was a tiny waif of a girl with no chest to speak of (both of which have changed drastically). I was also very shy and often hid in my room when family visited. Any kids who came to the house with family came to my room, where I hid in the shadows like Gollum in *The Lord of the Rings*. I'm kidding...sort of.

There were a few things, in particular, that gave me great joy as I was growing up. I loved sewing, drawing and painting, and I still do them fairly regularly. I loved reading and watching movies about whales (my favourite animal). I also loved Christmas. It wasn't about the gifts, it was everything else that came with it—the sights and sounds, and, of course, the smells! However, I think it always went deeper than that, and if there is a "Spirit of Christmas," then I think that's what I was obsessed with the most...the feel of the season.

My family still remembers one year my grandma was frustrated with untangling the tree's Christmas lights and I felt the need to interject.

"Grandma, you shouldn't get mad on Jesus' birthday!"

Was I for real? You betcha!

Another joy was music and theatre. I was introduced to my love of theatre when I first heard Andrew Lloyd Webber's *The Phantom of the Opera*. I received the Highlights of the London Cast Recording on cassette tape on Christmas Eve in the seventh grade, and I was hooked. The music from that show, along with Meat Loaf's *Bat Out Of Hell II* got me through depression in junior high. By the time I reached high school, I was in voice lessons and involved in the school musical *Fiddler on the Roof*, which we performed in April 2000. It was a chorus role, but I had the time of my life. I've had a deep appreciation for the Jewish roots of Christianity ever since that show. It helped me understand it more and started me on the road to coming out of my shell. I didn't hide from family anymore, and my shyness issues seemed to fade for the most part. I even went on to do more shows over the next few years. Mostly musicals, though I did play Iris in Shakespeare's *The Tempest* during the summer of 2002. I'd been interested in Shakespeare since I read *Macbeth* at twelve years old. I guess I was an odd child. I'd later watch the Roman Polanski movie based on the play. That, let me tell you, is an experience.

Though I performed on stage, I had a bad anxiety disorder. I suffered from full-blown panic attacks about a week before I was to start twelfth grade. I was often an anxious kid, but things had gotten worse; I headed to the family doctor.

He had initially tried putting me on an antidepressant, which made me feel nauseous and more panicky. I wound up in the emergency room of St.

Clare's Hospital, where I was given Ativan. When I returned to my doctor, he said he would put me on clonazepam because it was "less addictive."

Ativan and clonazepam are in the same class of drugs called benzodiazepines. Clonazepam had a longer half-life, so it was a little less addictive. What he didn't explain to me was the difference between addiction and physical dependency. Unbeknownst to me, I developed a physical dependency on this medication that I only took as prescribed. Back then, they figured they needed to up the dose if the drug no longer controlled the anxiety. It really means that your body has reached physical tolerance, and you need more to get the same effect. I went from the smallest dose (0.125mg) to, eventually, 2mg. It doesn't sound like a lot, but it's potent. For instance, 0.5 mg of clonazepam is equal to about 10 mg of diazepam (Valium).

In my early twenties, I started frequenting church again. I married a man who lived in another province and was heavily involved in his church's worship team. I was honestly way too young and had known him only a short time when we decided to get married. It was just pure stupidity on my part. I remember calling the pastor who was going to marry us when I was getting cold feet. All he said was that I would need to make up my mind soon because the women of the church would need to know whether to make the food for the reception or not. Thanks, Pastor! You were a *big* help. Really! I was young and needed some wisdom, and this is what I got. So I ended up marrying for all the wrong reasons. I moved away for a while with him, returned home again (with him), and found myself deeply unhappy in the relationship. It was very neglectful.

He came home from work one day gushing about another woman, flattered that she told co-workers that she thought he was "hot." This woman was known for having AIDS and not informing her sexual partners. He knew this, yet still found it flattering for some reason. I had tried to talk to him many times to try and repair the marriage, but he never took me seriously until I finally said I was leaving him. Even then, I don't think he truly meant it and would have returned to his previous behaviour in time. I later found out he'd also hit on a friend of mine while we were engaged.

"So what? I like redheads," he told me later, admitting it was true.

This was a significant turning point in my walk in the Christian faith; it was very hard on me. I felt like a failure for divorcing because of what the Bible says about it, and I ended up leaving the church. I couldn't reconcile getting divorced with being right with God, but I felt that spending the rest of my life with this person would be a huge mistake. Another big issue for me was the hypocrisy I saw around me in the church. What was so profoundly hurtful was when a few people seemed to take his side without asking me anything about mine. I left both him and the faith, feeling there was no place for me there. I blame myself because I was much too young to know better.

After this, I turned to paganism and the New Age. In my teens, I'd seen various things about it and felt drawn to it, but fear had kept me away. I got involved with a man who believed similarly. We dated for a couple of years and eventually, I re-married. I was living in the States away from everyone I knew and completely isolated with him and his parents. He, too, had lied to me until after we got married. I didn't have much luck regarding honesty from men in those early years. He'd tried things with his ex and lied to me about it for two years before tying the knot. He had eventually convinced me I was worrying over nothing when I said something felt "off," but then waited until four months after our wedding to tell me the truth. I developed a very crippling insecurity after discovering this, and I honestly stayed because, in my mind, I couldn't have two divorces. The one was bad enough. Even though I was no longer a Christian, I still felt I should try to make it work. Not long after, he began acting violently with me when I questioned him about things (and I had a lot of questions). I remained married and lived with him for another seven years.

During those first few years, we did a lot of travelling by car up and down the east coast. I even once took part in an audition to become a

Disney face character in Florida. Hey, it was an experience! I also got to visit the "National Christmas Center" in Pennsylvania which I just loved. Most years we went to see Trans-Siberian Orchestra in the lead-up to Christmas. Christmas rock? I was in! I still miss that particular tradition. It was all rockers with long hair, pyro, cherry pickers hanging over the audience and Christmas spirit. If you ever get the chance to see them, do it!

By late 2012 I had developed some strange digestive symptoms, so I quit gluten and dairy (which seemed to be the go-to suggestion of people at the time). Unfortunately, nothing seemed to help. I've even made morbid jokes on and off that my digestive system is homicidal (I guess technically suicidal).

At eight months old, I had an intussusception. That's an obstruction of the bowel where it folds into itself like a collapsing telescope. I was screaming in pain if anyone touched my stomach, vomiting, and listless. They'd even done a spinal tap on me to check for meningitis, and I didn't scream or cry for that...I was that tired and miserable. For one reason or another, it took a couple of days before they finally figured it out and performed surgery on me. I still have a scar that's a few inches long on my lower right abdomen.

In grade six, I'd again become very sick, and we had no idea why. Classmates thought I was bulimic as I'd been chubby and lost a lot of weight. It went on for months. There I was, almost thirty years old and feeling stomach sick again. So it's become a morbid running gag at this point.

Many later told me they felt it was nerves caused by my living situation, and maybe some of it was. I couldn't find any answers and became paranoid that maybe my anxiety medication was no longer agreeing with me. Not realizing any better, I went off them cold turkey. Luckily, I never had a seizure (which is common if you go cold turkey, as with alcohol), but I continued to get worse.

It turns out that I was in what they call a protracted withdrawal. I ended up doing things like using progesterone cream during this time, and progesterone works on the same receptors in the body. I didn't realize it was an issue, but I, unfortunately, found that out later when I accidentally made

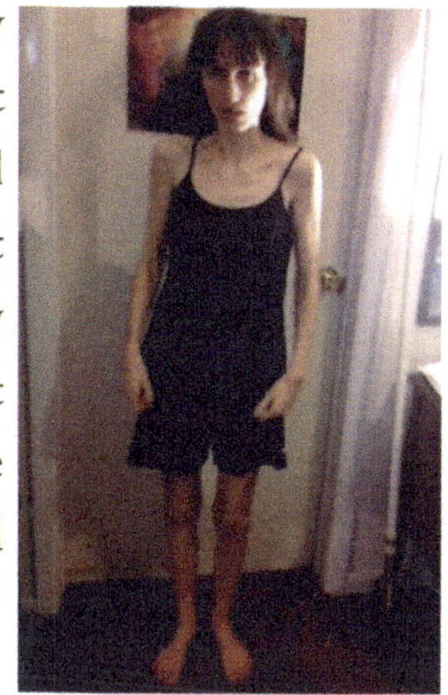

myself worse. For over a year, I went through a battery of tests, but everything was a dead end. I didn't know for sure at the time that it was a withdrawal issue, but it eventually landed me in the hospital. At my worst, I was so sick that I was 82 pounds, low on potassium, dehydrated, and on an IV and heart rate monitor in the hospital. During the bulk of the time that I went through this illness, my ex-husband would often ask me if we could commit suicide.

"Can we leave yet?" he'd ask.

As much as I was miserable trying to eat with a lack of appetite (even ice chips made me get sick sometimes), I was stubborn and refused to let the temptation to end it get to me. I'm glad I didn't listen.

I was put back on clonazepam eventually, but I am now working with doctors to very slowly ween off them as I don't want to have to take them for the rest of my life. I was also diagnosed with Lyme Disease and Bartonella while investigating why I was so sick and even discovered at some point I'd had West Nile Virus. Who knew? I was poked with so many needles for over a year trying to figure it all out, but it seems it was withdrawals all along.

In February 2014, I woke up one day to find out about the sudden death of a friend of mine from Toronto. He was thirty-six years old and had suffered a massive heart attack. I'll never forget the Sochi Winter Olympics because of it. The first half of 2014 was a pivotal point for me between his death and my nearly dying the following summer. I took a long overdue look at everything, and after a few more years of inner turmoil on the matter, I went home. I was home only three months when my grandfather, who'd helped to raise me, passed away a few days after having a stroke.

My ex-husband told me before I left that no one would want me after two divorces, which was of course my big fear. It was the same thing I'd worried about only four months after our wedding. I didn't care anymore. I wanted peace.

I left my ex and came back to Newfoundland in April 2017. This didn't happen without a considerable blow up, and his parents had to eventually call the police. He had become very angry about my planning to leave. I tried to call 911 as he was coming aggressively toward me, but he grabbed the phone. I wouldn't let go, so he twisted my wrists around violently and proceeded to try to smash the phone once he got it. His parents intervened while he was screaming at all of us. They told me to go upstairs while he ran off in his car. I then went to do a report at the police station where I got a temporary restraining order until I returned home. Before leaving, I had to face him in court. I thought I'd throw up. It was a very hard day. Ironically, I became great friends with his ex-girlfriend (who I'd met before) a couple of years after I came home. She'd dealt with PTSD from how he treated her as well and we've been a support to each other ever since. Shout out to Ange!

When I returned to Newfoundland, I dealt with many issues personally and some clearly didn't understand the gravity of what I'd just experienced. They didn't understand why I was so down at that time. Trying to work through everything that had happened and the failure of a second marriage was not easy.

I moved into a house with roommates in May 2017. And though they were all men, it wasn't at all weird. In October, a new roommate entered the house. On the first day, we bonded over a love of Christmas, and I showed him my plastic bin full of vintage decorations, which he seemed in awe of. We even talked about spiritual stuff and he showed me a rosary that used to belong to his mom who had passed. It became apparent over time that my new roommate had many drug issues, though I never saw him doing any myself. There was a time he was going to watch a movie with me, and he had to head back to his room to go to sleep because he was on Ativan or Xanax or something. One of those fast-acting benzodiazepines. By the winter, he was doing whippits in his room and stumbling around the apartment. Whippits are when you snuff the nitrous oxide out of a can for a cheap high. It's dangerous even for those who are otherwise healthy, and he wasn't. I'd hear crashes coming from his room across from mine and often didn't want to leave my room because I was scared of what I'd see. I could hear him talking to himself, and the nitrous oxide would lower his voice. When I say lower, I mean really low. He almost didn't sound human.

We were all concerned he was going downhill and discussed it with the property manager; she felt he would kill himself accidentally because he also had heart issues and she felt his body wouldn't be able to handle it.

Well, I hadn't heard anything from him one day the following May, and it was unusually quiet. One of my other roommates and I decided to check on him after I'd knocked on his door and not received any reply nor heard any movement. My other roommate opened the door, and when we peeked into the room, he was lying on his side with his face down in his baseball cap. I immediately began to panic when he wouldn't answer us. When I called 911, they asked us to get him on the floor to provide CPR, but when my roommate moved him, it was apparent that rigor mortis had already set in. He'd been dead for hours. This was my first real experience with someone who dealt with heavy addiction issues. He was a sweet guy, but he met a sad end and deserved better. He still crosses my mind.

During this time, I had entered into a new relationship with someone who was emotionally abusive. We'll just call my boyfriend at that time Damien. Mark and I got to know each other after he started talking to me about horror movies. So if anyone is familiar with old horror movie characters, you'll understand where Damien comes from. Because, well, that relationship was a horror show. It turned out the psychological damage I'd suffer would be way worse than what I'd endured physically in the past. I felt like a frog on a hot plate as you slowly turn up the heat. I will stop short of referring to him as a narcissist because the term gets thrown around these days, but the pattern of devaluing and then hoovering me back in was constant.

He would often use my previous traumas as weapons to hurt me more. It started very early on. I can't even begin to describe how many tears I cried during that relationship. Many times he'd invite me over and then act cruel, causing me to have to leave in the middle of the night. Why did he invite me at all? Sometimes he got mad that I was there, but he was the one who invited me over. I couldn't take it. Half the time, he would ask me to stay as I got ready to leave, but I was having no part of it. Then he'd accuse me of running and call me a "flighty bitch." One time he told me I was "too fat to get raped" and my weight became a common topic after a while. Another time, as I was leaving his place in the middle of the night after an episode of his, he shoved me lightly as I walked down his steps, though luckily, I was holding on to the railing.

"Aerobics, bitch!" he said as he closed the door behind me.

He liked my body enough to have his way with it, so I don't know. The worst part of all this is that I believed him. I did feel I was overweight, so I guess I felt he was right, and I somehow deserved it. The reality is no one deserves to be talked to like this, but in my mind he was just telling the truth. If anyone else had been in this relationship, I would have told them to get out of it quickly.

When I think back on it, I don't believe he knew what he wanted. I cannot fathom why I stayed as long as I did or why I moved in with him. I had toxic beliefs back then. I thought I'd know for sure whether we would work out or not if we lived together, but the answer was already obvious. My good friend Jen, from Ohio, had asked me if I'd consider dating him when I had first met him. My first gut reaction was, no way in hell. There was zero interest in him in that way at first. What drew me to him was that he seemed to have similar interests, though half of these turned out to be a lie in the end.

He told me more than once, even while not arguing, that my ex was right and that no one would want to marry me after two divorces. It was very hurtful. He criticized everything about me, from my art to my family and friends. Why was he even with me? The red flags had been there from nearly day one. I used to wonder why women stayed in abusive relationships, and now I've experienced different kinds myself. You truly don't understand it till you've been there. It's sad, but it's true.

Damien wasn't present for the physical abuse I'd been through in my past but constantly compared it to what he went through with one of his exes. It was as if it was a competition to him of who had it worse. He'd often make fun of me for what happened the last night I was with my ex and would downplay it.

"Oh no! He twisted your wrists!"

I had told him, in detail, the various things that had been done to me over the years, various acts of violence and putting holes in the walls, breaking down doors multiple times, and even smashing a window. He conveniently forgot all the things I'd told him. This was causing me to have to re-live that trauma over and over every time that I felt I had to correct him as he attempted to invalidate my experiences. The reality was, he had never forgotten any of it, I'm sure. So my constantly reminding him of what he'd "forgotten" was pointless in the end. This was a deeply traumatizing relationship for me, and I still deal with the scars to this day. Like I said, even more so than the ones from the previous relationship. The bulk of this one was psychological, and it messed with my head. It creeped me out that he often knew precisely what I feared without me telling him and then would say it. He admitted it had always been something he was "good" at. That's not a talent I'd be proud of. He admitted that he'd also said cruel things to his exes as if it somehow made this okay.

I don't want to make it sound like we never had any good times. We did, but they were often destroyed by the things he'd say to me. It never took too long for it to get bad again, and the bad outweighed the good. Sad to say, even with the pain I went through in my other relationships, this one had the lowest ratio of good times to bad. Which, is depressing, to say the least.

It's honestly disturbing to me how hard it had been in my life to find a genuinely kind man who loved me for me. All of them are people who honestly had it pretty good in their lives compared to Mark, yet he was the only one who treated me well. Sometimes, I guess, you appreciate things more when you've been in a bad way.

Before I left Damien, I had begun working at Marie's Mini Mart on Water Street in St. John's. This was where I met Mark, but I want to make something clear...nothing ever happened while I was still with Damien. Mark and I were friends a good chunk of the time that I knew him. But the worse things got with my ex, the more my feelings for Mark came forward.

I've made a point to emphasize my past relationships in this chapter because of how shocking it is to me that men who had it pretty good could be so messed up, but the one who didn't have it so easy was wonderful. Considering what my track record was like with men, I'm surprised I had the guts to tell Mark my feelings at all.

Some days you almost want to wallow in some form of hate when you still deal with the psychological damage caused by people in your past, but I believe forgiveness is a choice. So, I pray every day that this process of forgiveness continues, but it doesn't mean I'll ever have anything to do with any of them again. Anything I talk about in this book relating to that previous relationship is purely for understanding what I was going through at that time. Nothing more. I wish for him to have a better life than he's lived so far, one hopefully filled with more respect for any new partner. If he can do that and learn to live his best life, then I am happy for him.

Mark had always been very sweet to me. When I finally told him how I felt, I realized I'd made the best decision of my life. You know you're in love when you have a fear of vomit, and you're in the hospital holding the plastic tub for him as he gets sick, it gets on your arm and you simply wash it off.

It's not romantic; it's real.

I've never had a relationship like this, with so much love that I stuck by him even when faced with some of my biggest phobias.

We treated each other as equals and loved unconditionally. I don't think I could have ever been able to do the things I did for him every day with anyone else. Every day, even if he was in the hospital, I'd leave work and then go to him. Even though I was stretched thin, I did it gladly and not because I felt I had to. I wanted to see him as much as possible. Being with him was the best decision I ever made, even with the cruel fact that he had to leave this world. I will maintain that to the day I die. It's true what they say...the best loves are the ones built on friendship and trust.

2 LOST BOY

Who is Mark? If ever there was a complicated question to answer. Mark was definitely not someone you could fit into a box. To those who didn't know him well, he was an addict, criminal and panhandler. To those who got to know him, he was a loveable, silly (albeit often misguided and unconventional) angel. Though I admit you may not quite see it yet till later in the story as he led a tough life.

I met Mark while at work. So he was first my customer, then my friend, and finally the love of my life.

Many who knew him over the years knew him as a promiscuous, drug-addled drunk who had run-ins with the law. For much of his life, he just didn't seem to care about his well-being at all.

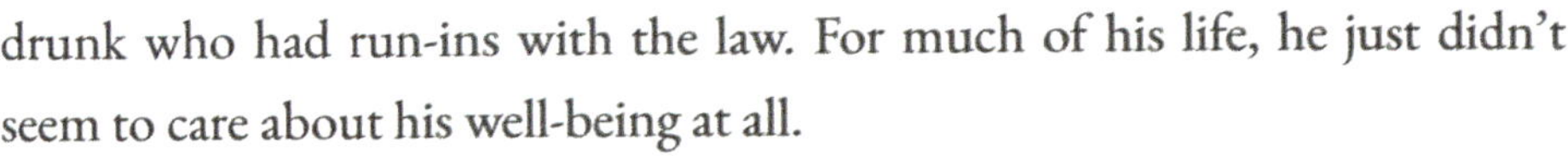

I didn't know what to make of him early on. But like anyone who truly got to know him, it became apparent to me in time that he had a sweet soul. It was undeniable once we became a couple.

Mark was born in Halifax, Nova Scotia, in the summer of 1980 and adopted at two days old. He admitted he was quite a little terror.

Personally, I'm shocked…kidding!

In 2017 as an adult, he'd written a novel about his life up to that point that he shared with people who knew him but has still gone unpublished. Some friends have asked if I would be publishing it, but with what I know about his feelings on it all towards the end of his life...it doesn't feel right for me to do it. By his own admission to me, he had many, many regrets, and I don't think he'd want them plastered for just anyone to read anymore. Sometimes we reach a new point in our lives where we have a different perspective, especially when faced with death. It's in the past, so I'm leaving it there. I feel that's what he would have wanted after the things he shared with me. This chapter includes snippets from what he wrote.

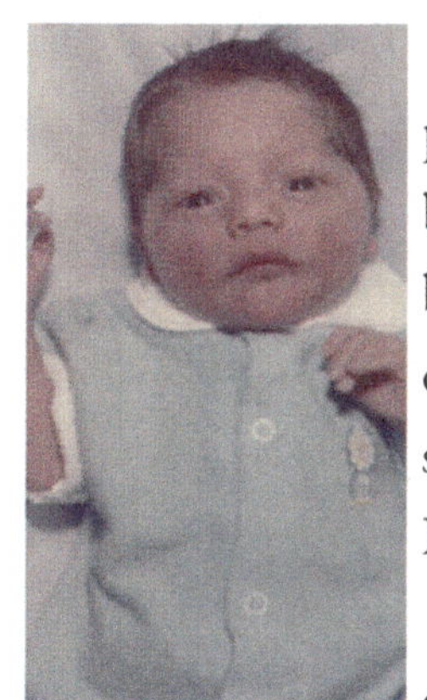

"I wasn't sexually abused or beaten like a lot of other people that I have met, but there was a lot of mental abuse between my mother and me. I don't know whether to blame her for the way I turned out, but she definitely did not help! I had every opportunity in the world to do something good with my life, but as you will soon learn, I always make the wrong choices."

I won't go into great detail about his family dynamics, only to say I was told some stories that are also not included in the book, and it's pretty heartbreaking. There are stories I know directly through him and some that his old friends have told me. Our mutual friends know of some pretty nasty things that happened outside of his family situation and that won't be discussed here. They are simply too private and disturbing. Some very concerning things happened when he was younger and as an adult. You experience a lot when you are on the street and involved with drugs. When you are dope sick, there's also a lot of stuff you'll do when desperate to get those drugs. Many lose their dignity during their fight to feel okay day to day.

Mark was brought up in a Wesleyan-Holiness church like I was. It was evangelical, and in a similar vein to the Salvation Army. I was told "he gave his life to Christ at eight years old" but fell away as a teen, as you will soon read. There were a lot of complicated circumstances that made him go in another direction in life. He had told me that hypocrisy was involved, among other things. I could relate to that big time after my own experiences.

As a child, he was involved in sports and loved hockey. He would get pumped up before going on the ice by listening to Mötley Crüe. Mark loved metal and rock, and he ended up getting into playing the guitar himself.

He estimated he was about ten years old when he began to get into trouble, and his family had decided to try putting him in a mental hospital in Halifax when he was about eleven.

“I was there for a seven-month evaluation that my social worker convinced my parents to stick me in there for. I remember going home on weekends, and they would bring me back on Sunday nights. I used to kick and scream not to go back to that place, but to no avail.”

He kept going back and, after all those months, was still deemed a “problem child.”

He detailed that up through his school years, he got into trouble to varying degrees. It ranged from breaking into a schoolmate’s house and stealing his parents’ liquor to taking the family car for a joy ride on more than one occasion. He even put WD-40 on the hinges of his bedroom door so his family wouldn’t hear him leave before going out.

“It turned out that when my dad went to work in the morning, the driver’s seat was still all the way up, and the stereo was full blast with fuckin’ Iron Maiden. Ha! I took my mom’s keys one day and went and made copies so I wouldn’t have to fuck around. She ended up taking her purse upstairs at night soon after. Little did she know!

I took the car a few times between there, but the worst was the time me and two friends took it for a spin. We were backing into poles, trees, over the curbs, and pretty much anything that was in our way. There was this rich neighbourhood we ended up cruising in called Portland Estates. We were driving around for a couple of hours causing shit and we were on the way home and at a top of a hill when I discovered that we had no brakes. It wasn't a huge hill but big enough you wanted brakes - that's for sure. Well, we didn't have much of a choice, so down we went. We made it around the corner without flipping (don't know how) and lo and behold there was a cop car right there. Shit - you can say that was the end of that joy ride! It turned out I was pressing on the gas and the brake at the same time so I burnt the brake pad to a crisp. All the backing into yards, over curbs, and into trees, the bottom undercarriage of the car was completely fucked."

After this particular spin in the car, he ended up being charged by his dad so he'd be able to get the insurance to pay for the damage. Mark said he did five months in Shelburne (a youth centre in Nova Scotia) for the incident. Throughout his early teens, he was in and out of group homes, and he said that was when he had first begun panhandling. He was mostly getting in trouble at school, skipping class and stealing small things like people's calculators and pens because he just wanted to annoy them. When I think about Mark in his school years, I can't help but think of the character Bender from *The Breakfast Club*. But he said that overall, he was a good boy by comparison before he decided to head out on the road.

"It was April 1996, and I was fifteen when I stuck out my thumb and hit the road to Toronto. I left with nothing but the clothes on my back and the twenty bucks my dad left me with on the side of the highway. I'd slept on the streets before but always in bank machines and never had any problems, but that was in Halifax, not Toronto. Years later, I asked my dad if he thought I would puss out and call for a bus ticket to come home. He said yes, but deep down, he knew I'd never be back. I hadn't really lived at home since I was ten, so they were used to me being gone anyway. I was so stoked when I hit the city limits of Toronto. I was fifteen, in Toronto, and fuckin' free to do what I wanted!"

Not long after he arrived, he made a couple of friends on the street and hung out with one of them for his first night in the city.

"That first night, I left to go find somewhere to sleep. We found some sleeping bags that someone had left, I tried to sleep outside, but it was too cold, so I ditched him and went and found a Tim Hortons and crashed on the bathroom floor. To be honest with you, I questioned my motives after that first night, but then the sun came and warmed the day."

Later, he bumped into his friend again, and he told Mark that he was going to squeegee cars, so Mark joined him.

"I remember the first light I did. I couldn't stop laughing. 'Really? Am I washing windows at a red light?' But the money was fuckin' good. I make better money than most people doing this, so laugh all you want."

He also began experimenting with harder drugs. It was mostly PCP that he used during those first days on the street.

"Man, I took too much. I was fucked up. I didn't know if I was coming or going! All we did all night was ride on the subway until it shut down. We ended up in this twenty-four-hour donut shop. Man, I'll never forget the smell in that place. Nothing but cigarette smoke, stinky homeless people, stale coffee and crack, which I didn't know at the time; it was fuckin bad! I think I was high for two days off that shit. I was tripping right out, and if I was coming down, I'd smoke a joint, and I'd be right back up there. I don't know how to describe the high from PCP, except you're just fucked. It makes everything look short; I remember thinking I could touch the top of the CN Tower. After the first couple of nights, I was tempted to go back home, but then I thought better of it. Nothing good could come of me going back home. From then on, it was nothing but fun!"

Eventually, he wound up in Montreal, and someone told him there was going to be a riot in Quebec City. So being high as a kite and a rebellious teenager, of course, he went!

"I found myself in jail. I was sentenced to two months for participating in a riot, which was well worth every minute because it was the best experience of my life. The juvie jail there was fun as hell. I was lucky that I was a juvie because people that were over eighteen were getting, like, seven years for that shit. Well, I did a month and a half there, then they sent me back to Nova Scotia to do the last two weeks. They sent me back because I was only sixteen, and they couldn't release me on my own. I also had a warrant in Nova Scotia for skipping out on my probation. I ended up in Waterville, N.S for my last two weeks.

When I got out, I thought for sure the cops would be waiting for me to get me for those warrants. But nope, they just gave me a bus ticket for Sydney, Cape Breton. I ended up only taking it to Halifax and then jumped on the highway; I was going back to Montreal. Fuckin' right I was!"

The following is one of my favourite stories he'd told me in person while at work, but he also documented it. It's heartbreaking now because we know alcohol took him from us, but the story and the dynamic with his "grampy" is cute.

"On my way back, I stopped at my grandparents' house in Moncton to say 'hi.' The funniest thing happened (for me anyway). I knew where Grampy had kept his liquor, well, since forever, but this time I took a 40 oz. of vodka. He kept it under the sink in the kitchen, and the bathroom was right there, so I grabbed the bottle, went in the bathroom, and mixed a drink. When it came time to put the bottle back, he was in the kitchen, so I had to hide it in the towels till later.

So, I take my drink and go downstairs to watch the hockey game and proceed to get wasted. I made a few drinks in between, but I needed a break after a couple, so I decide I'm going to go down the road to Tim Horton's to get a coffee, leaving my half-drunk glass hidden under the bed downstairs.

So, I go get a coffee, and when I get back downstairs, my grandfather had my drink on the table. He says to me, 'Pretty strong drink you have there, Mark.' He tells me if I just give him his bottle back, I can have another one when I finish that one. So, I tell him why I couldn't put it back earlier and go to the bathroom to get it and give it to him. Well, when I finished my drink and asked for another, he told me I'd had too much! Fucker blackmailed me! After the fact, I found it funny. Out of my whole family, my dad, grandparents, aunt, and brother are the only ones I care about or talk to. My grandparents died ten years ago; if there's a heaven, they're in it.

I ended up getting into a fight with some neighbourhood kids the next day and got beat up, but my grandmother refused to call the cops. That's how awesome she was, by saying 'Mark will only get in trouble.' That was a solid woman right there!"

When Mark returned to Montreal, he "met the Devil" (as he put it). It was the first time he shot up cocaine.

"And it was the beginning of a life of me being trapped in a bottomless pit that I still, twenty-one years later, haven't climbed out of yet. I started staying up for ten days straight, eating nothing but maybe a peanut butter sandwich from a drop-in centre called the Bunker, or a few donuts from the dumpster across the street from the hotel/shooting gallery where I ended up staying at."

He eventually made his way to Vancouver, somewhere he had intended to visit for years. "All I really remember when I first got into Vancouver was that it was a really nice day and I thought to myself, 'wow this place is really something else,' looking at the skyscrapers with the Rocky Mountains in the background. I was super happy to be there. When I was twelve years old, I was in jail for three months for a break and enter, but I was going to school while I was there. One day I found a book on 'the shelf,' and it had a picture of downtown Vancouver on it. I said to myself that day in class that I was going to go there one day, and here I was looking at what I was pretty much looking at four years ago in that book! It was awesome."

From there, he hopped on his first freight train. It was headed to Washington state.

"I will never forget this till the day I die. The sound of that powerful engine shaking the ground beneath my feet, the smell of the railroad ties, the sound of steel on steel, and the adrenaline running through my body.

I said to Lenny, 'This is us, fucker,' waited for the engines to pass, found a grainer, and jumped on. What a rush!"

Mark loved to listen to metal music...but really, Mark *was* metal!

This was the beginning of years of train-hopping all over North America and he even spent some time in Mexico. He loved travelling and saw more than most of us ever will in our lives.

"I crossed the two countries riding freight trains and hitch-hiking before I was eighteen," he said.

When I named this book *Runaway Train*, it seemed so fitting for him. It also makes me think of the song by Soul Asylum we all knew growing up. The music video shows different scenarios of kids ending up on the streets or lost. Every time I hear it, I think of him.

Besides cocaine and drinking, he also began to use heroin during his travels. Previously he'd been against heroin and had given people a hard time about it.

"There was a saying back then, 'Punks not junk.'"

When he first tried it, he said it hadn't appealed to him at all the first few times that he'd done it. That changed with time. He also wound up having a problem with, of all things, benzodiazepines. Not only that...but clonazepam like what I'd taken for years. Mark didn't take these as prescribed, however. He documented a little about his struggle with them.

"This guy and I get to talking, and the conversation turns to drugs. I tell him I have some coke, and he tells me he has a bottle of 2mg clonazepam, so we decide to do a trade.

Let's back up here a second, and I will tell you this: I have a really big problem with benzos, and I know more than anything in this world that I should not take these fuckin' things, but I do, and I always end up blacking out in a bad fuckin' way."

It was ironic to me he'd abused these on and off. It's no wonder that with everything that he bombarded his body with, it eventually gave up. Not once during the time that we knew each other did he ever ask me for any of mine, nor did he abuse any of the pills that he had been prescribed. And as you can see, he abused many different kinds of drugs for years.

"I had gotten ahold of some acid, but no one wanted to do any with me, so I found myself tripping out at four in the morning all by myself," he wrote. "I stumbled upon a jerrycan, three-quarters full of gas, and thought it would be a good idea to huff some. So, I start huffing, and the next thing I know is that there are balls of fire shooting out of the top of the jerrycan, bouncing off the walls, telling me that I'm going to die. 'You're going to die! You're going to die!' So, I throw the jerry can out the backdoor yelling at the top of my lungs, 'fuck no, not me!'"

His most intense trip on acid was when he once went to get McDonald's while tripping and said that the cashier's face briefly turned into the face of a lizard.

As you can see he had many crazy experiences, though they were not all to do with drugs and alcohol. Mark had been to many of the big cities in the U.S. One story he told was of a scary incident at Cabrini-Greens in Chicago. The housing project had been infamous for its crime and had started as public housing for less fortunate families. It wasn't always a bad place, but it deteriorated due to various societal issues and neglect. Most of it got torn down years ago.

"The only thing I knew about Chicago at the time was that Lenny had been there and had gotten dropped off in this housing project called Cabrini-Greens, and was shot at! HA!

I had no clue where everyone would be hanging out, but the guy that had picked me up dropped me off on Belmont and Clark and told me that's probably where I would find the likes of myself, and he was right. He also told me that they had stopped delivering mail in Cabrini-Greens, because the gangsters were squeezing rounds off at the mailman. Just another day in the ghetto!

I ended up going into the Greens one day to get a ten-piece. I found some crackhead to take me in for five bucks. Well, that place didn't disappoint. In terms of...get the fuck out of there fast! I had to walk up five flights of stairs and when I got to the top, there were three dudes sitting on milk crates with red bandanas around their faces. There were two guys standing on the side of another dude with a plastic shopping bag filled with nickel rocks, and they each had 9s. I didn't have a problem, but when I was leaving, this ten-year-old girl started throwing a bike tier at me yelling, 'get out of here, white boy.' It was funny, but I didn't dare utter a word. They should make a t-shirt, stating, 'I SURVIVED CABRINI-GREEN'S!'"

During all of this addiction and travelling, he fell in love for the first time. He was only in his teens at that time, and she was three years older than him. To say she did a number on him would be an understatement. She was his first love and first colossal heartache. This girl cheated on him numerous times during their travels together, and from then on until we got together when he was forty years old, he still dealt with paranoia about getting cheated on. One time he detailed walking in on her and his friend getting out of the shower together. Of course, a fistfight ensued. He ended up staying in the bathroom, crying and burning pictures while angry and hurt when he heard moaning from the other room. Of course, things escalated, and they started fighting again. I remember at one point (I can't remember the exact moment this came up now), he told me about his temper when he gets hurt in that way. He pretty much said (in a non-threatening way, mind you) that when he loses it, he *really* loses it and how scared he was of being hurt again. I told him it was a non-issue. I'd never do anything remotely close to what she did to him. Even after that incident, they still went back and forth with each other, and she even ended up pregnant with twins. He was eighteen years old, and she ended up having an abortion before continuing to cheat. He finally had it one day and left. I never asked him, so I don't know if this thought ever came into his mind, but it occurred to me that there was always the *possibility* the babies were not even his anyhow, considering her unfaithfulness. We'll never know.

He allowed himself to become very vulnerable with me, and I knew it was scary for him. He'd not had many serious relationships after her in his life due to how that relationship affected him. He took a risk on me, and I'm so happy he did. One of our local friends, Barry (his name has been changed for the book, and you'll be hearing more from him yet), spilled to me one day just how much I meant to Mark, which I'll detail later. As much as I'm happy I was able to have him for myself as a result of him and this former girlfriend breaking up...it still breaks my heart that she'd hurt him so much. I understand that kind of damage. I still have scars too as I said earlier. The fear came up multiple times with us...enough that I knew he was just as scared as I was of being hurt. A friend he'd had since childhood told me she couldn't understand why he kept getting back together with that girlfriend. As I've said, I've been in toxic relationships myself. I get it to some extent. There's a fear in ripping the band-aid off and saying enough is enough sometimes. You become somewhat used to being mistreated.

During all the years he was on the road, he also lost many friends to overdose or suicide. That's got to play on someone's mind. As I said before I still think of my friend who died doing whippits. Mark knew many people who had died untimely deaths. Again, mental health and trauma have a big hand in addiction, so it's no shock to know many he knew had died the same kind of way. There's got to be better help out there somehow. I don't know what the answer is, but I wish I did. It seems like the issues in the world just keep growing with no end in sight. Whether it's street drugs or prescribed drugs like benzodiazepines and opioids, many either deal with these issues in some respect or know someone who does. Everyone talks about the COVID pandemic but not enough people are aware or trying to properly help the current pandemic of addiction that exists across the globe.

Mark eventually landed back in Montreal and got into heaps more trouble out there. So much so that he was no longer allowed to step foot in Quebec or he'd be arrested. He eventually headed east, here to Newfoundland. He'd been here before, back in 2009. No surprise he got in trouble here too. That time, he stole beer from a gas station.

"The next day in court, I got thirty days. The whole second page of the paper had my picture and had big bold letters at the top of the page saying 'HOMELESS MAN STEALS BEER' with a big article written. It was like I was going to the electric chair or something! I guess they had nothing else for news that day, it was fuckin hilarious."

It was upon his return to the province a few years later that his worst run-in with the law occurred and why his life began to change. He went to prison for over a year after stabbing someone in the shoulder while blacked out on drugs and alcohol. He'd also slashed his wrists at the same time. As horrific as this was, it was not in his nature to do such a thing. These drugs had him out to lunch, and he was deeply sorry for what had happened. It was a huge reality check for him in many ways. It was said that prison had changed him a great deal. When he got out, he continued to panhandle in the downtown area of St. John's, usually in front of Marie's, where I'd be going to work eventually.

When I first met him, he had his brown curly hair grown out very long and poking out from under a baseball cap. I often joked he reminded me of Lieutenant Dan in *Forrest Gump* after he returned from the Vietnam War, but with legs, obviously. He was wearing a Pink Floyd vest (he later had the patches changed to Iron Maiden) and the most striking blue eyes I had ever seen. I mean, really, really blue. Who was this wild man buying beer and cigarettes from me?

Beer was not actually his poison of choice. That title went to vodka. White Russians, actually. It was that poison that eventually took him from us.

As you've now read, Mark dealt with addiction to all kinds of drugs throughout his forty-one years. Heroin was terrible for him. He said as a general rule, he knew after using it three times, he'd be hooked again. He hated that his dealer "had him by the balls." That's a direct quote of his, of course. He had a colourful way of speaking at times. But it was alcohol and not heroin, he said, that was the most insidious for him personally, and yet so normalized in our society.

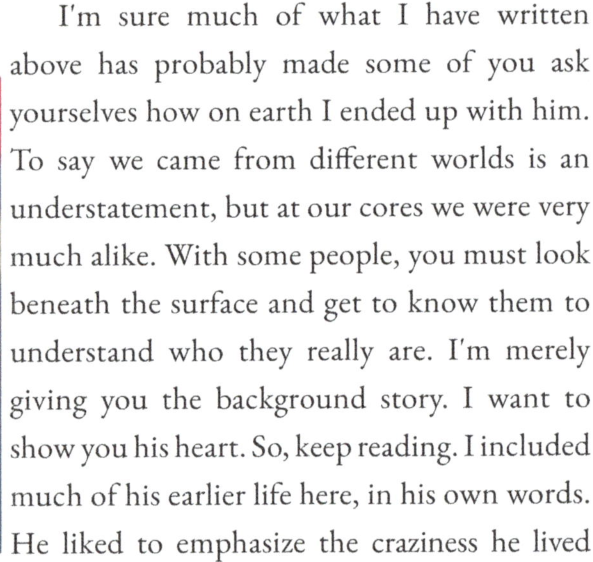

I'm sure much of what I have written above has probably made some of you ask yourselves how on earth I ended up with him. To say we came from different worlds is an understatement, but at our cores we were very much alike. With some people, you must look beneath the surface and get to know them to understand who they really are. I'm merely giving you the background story. I want to show you his heart. So, keep reading. I included much of his earlier life here, in his own words. He liked to emphasize the craziness he lived through, but he had a huge heart. Friends have compared us to tales of unlikely pairings like *Beauty and the Beast* and *Lady and the Tramp*, which I find a little funny but also very appropriate. Many know his crazy life stories, but there is so much more to his complicated soul. He would give you the shirt off his back if you needed it.

We gave each other so much love. The type of love we both wanted and on some level, needed. He did nothing but enrich my life, and I am better for having known and loved him.

3 ACCIDENTALLY IN LOVE

In August 2020, I was finishing up a couple of months of training at another Marie's Mini Mart location before being sent downtown to Water Street. I had requested that location as I was living with my mother and stepfather at that time, and my boyfriend and I were about to move in together in the downtown area in September. I had wanted to live downtown for as long as I could remember. I'm not sure of my exact reason, but I just loved the atmosphere and the idea of being near the harbour. I never knew how much my life would change because of working there.

Above left: My friend Yvonne created this painting of the store, and I wanted to include it with her permission.

I wouldn't be able to tell you the exact moment I met Mark. I was a little nervous as I'd be working shifts alone, but I knew that's what it would entail beforehand. Nervous or not, I was looking forward to it. At the other location, I had always worked with someone else. I was timid for the first little bit as I got used to the store. Very soon after arriving, I found out we had a regular group of panhandlers who hung around outside. I wouldn't get to know some of them until much later because they were not allowed in there due to things they'd done in the past and were banned.

There were a couple down there that I did not like who treated me awful, but most of them were very friendly. The same went for the other regular customers. There were some bad apples, but for the most part, I met many lovely personalities there. It's funny how quickly you get to know what brand of cigarettes or beer someone is about to ask for.

Later, the guy who showed me the ropes at work when I moved down there found out about Mark and me before I left. He'd left to move to another location very early on and had been in the store visiting. He told me out of all the people downtown, he trusted Mark the most. He said he'd trust him with his life. Out of all the panhandlers, I do recall noticing Mark. As I said previously, he stood out to me with his long dark curls and big, very blue eyes.

But my first real memory of him that sticks out was one evening when he came in drunk, trying to open the beer cooler off to the left of my cash register. I was busy with customers, and he grabbed the handle and kept jiggling the cooler as he didn't realize it was latched in his inebriated state.

There was a latch on it because the cashier was the only one who was supposed to go into it. He looked pretty comical as he stood there shaking the cooler, trying to open it.

"I'm supposed to grab whatever you want," I reminded him.

He said he was just trying to save me time where it was busy so that he'd already have it in hand. Supposedly. Ha!

Above left: From a picture I'd taken of the view out of the store window in September 2020. I never even knew until after Mark passed that he was in the corner of it.

After that, there were a blur of random interactions for the first couple of months. People often complained about them panhandling outside, but if I'm honest, I felt safer with them there. Within the first few weeks of working there, my wallet got stolen from my bookbag in the back room; and a couple of months later, I got robbed. No, not by any of them. Just the joys of working at a convenience store!

Mark would come in at random and make conversation with me. I think the first time I can recall, he asked me if I'd seen the movie *The Exorcism of Emily Rose.* Isn't that a romantic way to recall your first conversation with the one you love? We talked about horror movies more than once. Of course, I laugh about it now.

He'd often say hello by shooting me the middle finger from outside the window, and I'd reply with the same thing causing him to show off his completely toothless laugh. He'd lost teeth due to years of drugs and alcohol and throwing up from it, not to mention living conditions on the street. He'd come in and tell me to look up random songs. One of which, *Yellow Listerine*, was...interesting. I also found out we both loved pirates, which was cool. During COVID he actually used a pirate skull bandana for his mask when he'd come in the store. In all honesty, while covered in all those tattoos and with his long curly hair, he reminded me of a pirate himself. He was weird and loveable. It was hard not to like Mark. Anyone who really got to know him, liked him.

One day, not long after I'd been robbed, Mark came in to tell me he was headed out to Harbour Grace for rehab. He said if anyone were to ask if I knew where he went, to let them know because he'd be gone about a month. I remember having a bit of a sad feeling that he wouldn't be around. That's not to say I knew I had feelings for him at this point, only that something was brewing. I definitely enjoyed his company and talking to him.

When he came home just before Christmas, he popped into the store sober as can be, in a wonderful leather jacket (that I now wear).

"Look at you!" I said, happily.

He looked pretty spiffy. I couldn't help but feel proud of him. I'll admit...I knew he looked good, and we'll leave it at that.

A couple of days later it was Tibb's Eve here in Newfoundland. It's known everywhere else as "Christmas Eve, Eve." In this province, it's a night that's notorious for getting absolutely plastered drunk. Our hours had been reduced during the fall, and I was closing around 7 pm. Damien had come to meet me to head to Dollarama to pick up some Christmas essentials. I'd stepped outside and saw him and Mark chatting when I locked up. Mark was absolutely sloshed, half hunched over, and pretty out of it. We spoke for a minute; I can't remember about what, then we crossed the street to head to the store.

I still remember walking away from Mark, and in hindsight, I keep yelling at myself to turn back, but that was the decision I made at the time. As we crossed the street, Damien piped up, saying, "He thinks the world of you."

I intentionally decided not to question him on this, but for one reason or another, I wanted to ask him what he meant and may have had an inkling something was starting for me then. I was nervous to ask the question for fear he'd pick up on something, *real or imagined* on his part. I couldn't even tell you for sure how I felt at this point.

That hadn't been the first time the two had met. Months before, Damien had met me downtown, and I'd forgotten to use the bathroom before locking up. When I went to use the bathroom across the street, Mark had stopped Damien, asking him if he wanted some weed, which he did. When I came out, and he told me he'd taken weed from Mark, I asked him if he was sure he wanted to smoke that. I knew Mark had used a lot of drugs over the years and I wasn't sure if it would be laced with something else. That was only a couple of weeks after I'd started working down there. It's comical to me in hindsight. Mark would later tell me he couldn't even remember meeting Damien. He knew about him from when we'd chat, but couldn't picture him at all.

Christmas came and went. During the winter everything slowed down, but the demise of my relationship with Damien was speeding up. The psychological trauma he was inflicting was only getting worse with time, and nothing I did was good enough to make the man truly love me. If I was quiet?

I was mumbling. If I was loud? It was too loud. If I ate too fast? He criticized me. I tended to eat faster after my illness, to make sure I got any calories into me before I possibly got nauseated...it seemed to be a trauma response. My body that he once deemed beautiful...well, now it was too fat. I got called Tony Soprano while wearing my bathrobe once, as he was bullying me. I didn't like who I was becoming in this relationship. I had started lashing out at him when he did not leave me alone or if he said something particularly nasty. I was going between a stressful work environment, then coming home to him rambling and barging into the bedroom at all hours when I needed to sleep. This was happening when I had to work the next day. It was not healthy, and I started to feel increasingly sick at work.

It wasn't nice stuff he'd barge in to say to me. While that would have been frustrating...at least it would have seemed like he was doing it because he loved me and wanted to talk to me. But no, it was just nastiness. He'd spew off awful things to himself in the living room, but within earshot. He'd say stuff to the cat about me, knowing full well I could hear him. His words hurt me deeply. I missed work a few times because I was kept up all night, and things were not looking good.

During all those months, I had a few people (not a lot) tell me to "Watch out for that Mark guy; he stabbed someone." This was true, as I detailed before. But honestly, after getting to know him, the only thing I could respond with in my head was, "Really? Mark? Yeah, ok." It just wasn't who he naturally was; that was obvious. I felt very comfortable with him and had for quite a while.

I will admit that at this point, I was starting to feel like maybe I had a secret I was hiding, but I was still sort of in denial.

In the meantime, Mark kept coming into the store to chat. On Saturday, the second of January, I was at work as usual when an unruly man entered the store. I think he may have been drunk, but I can't be sure. He complained to me about the panhandlers. He called them garbage or trash or something in that vein. He ended up being very rude to me. I'd just had a bottle of milk with a snack and was clearing my throat for a bit afterward. There's a reason why my old voice teachers used to tell me not to drink milk before singing!

Below left: Mark squeegeeing a car across the intersection from the store.

Anyhow, anytime I cleared my throat, he'd mimic it in a demeaning tone. He spoke to me in a demanding voice, asking rudely for cigarettes while roughly throwing his food down on the counter. I tried telling him I had a right to refuse service if he continued disrespecting me, so he said he was sorry. Then he put his items into the paper bag, and it tore. He flipped and threw it over the counter at me and onto the floor. He grabbed his stuff and almost forgot his cigarettes on the counter. I called out to remind him. It's not that I even wanted to be helpful, I just didn't want to risk him having to come back in after he left.

After he went outside, I saw him briefly mouthing off to someone sitting in front of the store. The wall was blocking them from my view, so I didn't know who it was. I grabbed the few tips I had on the register and went out to see who was there. It was Mark!

"Did he just harass you?" I asked, crouching down next to him

"Yeah," he responded.

"He can say what he wants, but you treat me with more respect than he did."

I tried to hand him the tips I had in my hand, but he wouldn't accept the coins. He seemed sober and kind of sad. I don't know exactly what was said to him, but he just seemed kind of done. I still don't know why he didn't accept my tips.

Within the next week, Mark was back to being silly again. He came in one evening, leaned on the counter, and showed me a video of himself on his phone, *almost* entirely naked except for his vest, a monkey hat, and a glove over his crotch. I started laughing.

"You're nuts, b'y!" was the only thing I could say to that. But that was Mark. I think he got a kick out of showing it to me.

"B'y" is a Newfoundland expression for boy. You can say it to anyone really, but it's hard to explain. If you're from here, you just get it.

I wouldn't doubt if he showed almost everyone that he knew that video because it was so ridiculous and funny. That's who he was...playful and weird, and it was wonderful. He even had this plastic toy gun he carried around, It was a dart gun but it was black and realistic looking with a suction cup dart. One day he was standing outside while I was working and he knocked on the window then shot the dart at the window, causing me to flinch for some reason even though I was behind the glass. He just laughed and laughed. I can't say I blame him. Like I said, he was such a silly, funny guy. It's what would make the news that would come later that much harder to hear.

Everything had died down after Christmas. During the slow days, I had a notebook on the counter that I was writing in between helping customers.

I was trying to come up with notes for a story I wanted to write. I'd written things in the past, but they *always* fell through, and I never went ahead with publishing. Some were loosely based on real life and usually based in the fantasy genre, but nothing ever came of them.

Mark came in one day when it was pretty dead. I had bought a notebook for myself that we carried in the store, and I was leaning on the counter thinking and writing notes. He asked what I was doing and when I told him, that's when he informed me about how he'd written a book about his travels and living on the street. I told him I was interested in reading it but never got to until much later.

I never thought in a *million years* I'd be writing a nonfiction instead of a fictional story. Let alone about this particular topic.

Life and love can be *really* strange.

4 BAD NEWS

By the beginning of spring, I'd noticed that Mark had disappeared on and off in spurts. St. John's was in the middle of one of our COVID lockdowns during the winter; but other than that, I wasn't sure what was going on. I was personally dealing with a lot at home. As of April, I'd started wasting money hiding at a local hotel for a night or two at a time to escape Damien. Saturday nights were especially hard for me, as I had to be up to open on Sunday mornings. My health and mental health were wearing thin with the increasing mental battering I was taking.

Mark still came in to talk when he was around. At some point when he came in, he told me a story about how he and Barry had been hanging out, and how Barry had apparently been egging him on to stab him in the hand for some reason.

So, he did.

I swear, the stories I heard about these guys...you'd think they were the Stooges. It wasn't severe, and everything was fine, but I guess it was a lesson in "be careful what you wish for." Mark seemed to think that if you are literally going to ask for it...be prepared to get it. He couldn't stop laughing at how dumb it all was as he relayed the story to me. So, he gave Barry what he wanted in this case, dumb request or not.

I'll never forget the day Mark told me he was sick. It was the fourteenth of April, though it didn't feel like it. It was still winter to me, as it was still so cold. Newfoundland has three seasons, not four, in my opinion...winter, summer, and fall. Anyhow, I had loved the story of the Titanic since I was a young child (the real story, not the movie...though the film does come up later), so the date always stuck out in my mind as it was the day it hit the iceberg. Oddly enough, it was also the day I left my ex-husbands home in 2017. It seems appropriate that I found out on that date.

He came into the store that afternoon, and I was happy to see him...but what he had to say was devastating. He revealed to me he'd been hospitalized four times in six months, then told me he had been diagnosed with stage 4 liver cirrhosis and had been told he was dying.

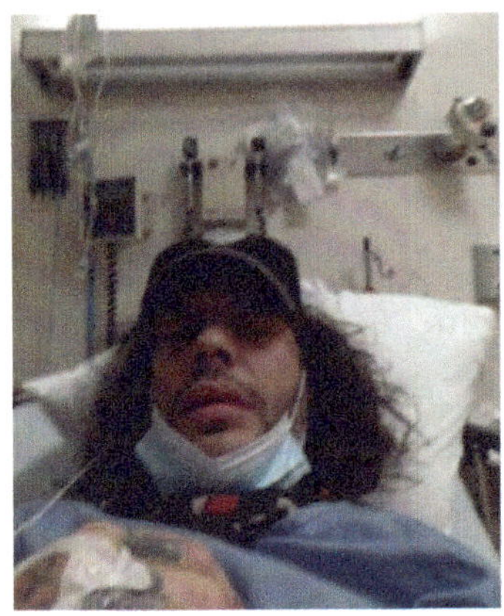

Later, during the summer, I'd come to find out he didn't realize stage 4 was the last. I guess the doctors had assumed he'd know. Maybe he did at this point; I'm not sure. I think he knew he was dying, but felt that he'd have more time than he did. Either way...the ship hit the iceberg. I felt crushed when I heard this; he was one of my favourite people. This was when he revealed to me that alcohol was the worst of all the drugs he'd done. We talked for a bit, and as he began to walk out the door, I felt the need to speak up.

"Take care of yourself...I know that's hard."

He came back further into the store again.

"I dunno, man," he continued as he mumbled something I couldn't make out while staring out the window. He looked contemplative like he wished things could be different. "People judge..." he continued as he motioned down at his clothes. I didn't see anything wrong with them (personally).

"Listen, you are the nicest person I've met down here," I told him.

As we talked, the reality of the situation hit me more and more. He seemed more than a little lost. I started to think about working there and him not being around, which really upset me. From that point forward, I began to not lie to myself anymore.

About a week later, Damien and I had a huge fight. He was keeping me up all night and saying a lot of vicious stuff, so I lost it. It was just earlier that month that I'd had to leave for the hotel because he'd put down everything about me, including my time in theatre. He also insulted my artwork. I was so upset. When he left the house to have a smoke, I took this mounted poster off the wall that my dad had done up for me when I was in the *Rocky Horror Show* in 2002. I went out to the kitchen and took a steak knife to it over and over while I was crying. I left it destroyed on the kitchen counter. He acted pleased by what I'd done to it when he came back in, and told me it was the best art I'd ever made. He said I could paint, but that I wasn't a "real artist." The destroyed poster was true art to him. I was in the bedroom bawling at hearing him say this. I had started crying after listening to him in silence as he went on and on, and I just finally cracked.

"What? I'm saying it's a beautiful piece of artwork that you did!" he said simply, as I sat in the bedroom crying about it.

I still can't get over that I put up with any of this treatment.

When I came out of my bedroom later, I saw that he had it stood up on the mantle. It was below paintings that he had insulted, ones I actually put work into. I went for a walk with it and threw it in a garbage can down the road. He had insisted he wanted to keep it, maybe as a prized reminder of the pain he caused me. It was all pretty twisted.

He had me in a state again now only a couple of weeks later. He'd again been cruel to me, going all that night and morning. I was extremely low on myself as is. I cracked again, so much so that the neighbours called the police because of the screaming. It was the only time in my life that the police had ever been called because of me. I was, and still am, so ashamed of it.

Cops came to the building often, but it was always for the upstairs neighbour I had at the time, not me. They informed me there is no law in the criminal code of Canada against emotional abuse (something I firmly believe should change after my experience). Apparently, people are just allowed to bully and tear others down emotionally. They also said it was best to stay apart for at least a few hours. I decided to stay at the hotel again to get a break, but not much changed with him when I got home.

Around this time, a tall and blonde young man came into the store asking if I'd seen Mark around. This was a little over a week after Mark had told me he was dying. He had just been in the store chatting to me and had left only a short time before this guy arrived. I let him know that Mark had said he was heading home.

He also asked me my name before leaving and informed me he's terrible with names and might have to keep asking me in the future. He told me his name was Jesse and that he had just arrived in town to visit Mark and then went to find him.

Little did I know this second scoundrel was about to become part of what would become my little family, as well. Almost every day after this, I saw them hanging out together in front of the store.

Above left: Jesse and Mark, late May 2021.

The next time he came in, he stopped and pointed at me with both pointer fingers.

"Krista?" he asked, but with an air of confidence.

I nodded. He got it right! Hooray!

I later found out the reason my name stuck out in his head was that pretty much from the moment he got here, he had found out Mark had feelings for me. If only I knew then. He had called Jesse up not long after he had told me his diagnosis, telling him he had to get his butt out here.

"I'm dying, man."

Over the next little while, I got to know him better, and we bonded over a love of *Doctor Who*. I grew up on the older episodes with Tom Baker and such, but I'd come back to it during the Eleventh Doctor, Matt Smith. As soon as I mentioned the show, he raised both arms in the air and yelled, "*Doctor Who*!" Yeah...he's definitely a fan! It's incredible how a show can span so many decades and capture generations of fans. He sounded as if he were at a sports game cheering when he said it, in all honesty.

Every time I saw Mark, I pined. My feelings had increased over the months, but now he was on a time limit, and that scared me. We were from two different worlds and it was almost as if that window was like a portal between us.

I found ways to catch a peek at him through the window when they'd be sitting outside the store. I found out later that apparently a couple of times Mark would try to catch a peek of me through the store window himself and Jesse would tease him about it. I had no clue. It's so funny to me we were both essentially doing the same things.

A memory came back to me from months before, when the owner of the building had been into the store. He had talked to me about the panhandlers and how many of them he'd known over the years. He informed me that, in his experience, they usually ended up dead. He'd pointed out Mark that day, saying, "That one...it's a lifestyle for him." In hindsight, it gives me the heebie-jeebies because it was almost like he foreshadowed the news that I had just received now in April.

So as the time ticked away and I was wasting energy trying to make a dead relationship work, I continued to chat with Mark and catch glimpses of him like a shy teenage girl from inside the store. A few times, I'd snapped a photo or a video clip. I wasn't trying to be a weirdo, but if he was going to die, I knew I wanted something to remember him by, even if it was something as small as a simple picture. It's funny because Mark never liked people taking his picture without permission. I know I got a pass because of the circumstances and because we loved each other. Somehow, he'd gotten into my heart over the months of weird, sometimes drunk interactions. He continued the habit of knocking on the window sometimes before he and Jesse would sit down and continued greeting me with the middle finger. I'd always return the gesture, and I'll admit that my heart would skip a beat anytime I watched him laugh as I did it back.

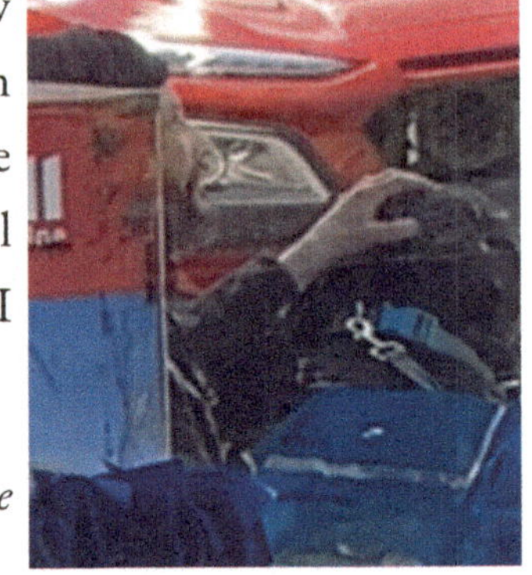

Right: Mark petting someone's dog while talking. Late May 2021.

One morning, there was a crowd of people outside the door to the store, waiting to grab their cigarettes and such before work. Mark and Jesse were further down near the sidewalk. I went out to unlock the door and let people in, I looked in their direction, right at Mark. Of course, that's where my eyes went! I couldn't help it! I can remember vividly that as soon as he looked over at me, he got that big toothless open-mouth smile again.

I still wonder if he noticed that I happened to be looking at him. He must have, as he was looking right at me. It didn't matter if he had teeth or not. He had an infectious smile and you couldn't help but smile back. His face would light up when he laughed. I still choke up all these months later when I see him laughing in my head.

One day he came in to use our microwave to warm up a cup of Kraft Dinner he'd bought at the dollar store, and I decided to ask him more about his family. He'd revealed they had a strained relationship, especially with his mom. He was very hurt that he'd tried calling her at Christmas and she had refused to speak to him; it turned out to be his last Christmas.

“It struck a fuckin’ bone with me, man,” he said. He seemed angry about it, but I could tell it hurt.

I had been wondering if he'd considered going to see them since he found out he was sick. but he hadn't for various reasons, that being one of them.

"They're just waiting for that phone call; they’ve been waiting for that phone call for years," he commented.

I was horrified when he said this. Sadly, no one ever did come to see him before he passed, though his father and brother stayed in contact over the phone a couple of times. I asked him if he had any idea why things were like that and he said he was the black sheep of the family.

“But you’ve tried to reach out and they just...”

“Shun me? Pretty much,” he continued quietly. "I had my mom drove grey by the time I turned six," he added with a laugh. Though I could tell from our conversation there was pain there.

Over the next couple of days, things fell apart more with Damien. Work, though stressful, was an escape.

One day Mark and Jesse were passed out in front of the store; and at first, no one could wake them up. The cops were called and they managed to wake them up finally and took them away.

The next afternoon, I was downtown before my usual Saturday evening shift and ran into Dollarama for some snacks to last me until the next day. Due to Damien keeping me awake with his nonsense, I was headed to the hotel (again) to waste more money. I just wanted to be able to get to work and not be a zombie the next day. He had already started with me that morning, so I knew it was inevitable.

I was about to cross Queen Street from Dollarama, when I saw Mark coming down the road. My heart jumped at the sight of him; so I called out to him, and we stopped to talk on the corner. I asked him what happened to them when the cops took them away the day before, and he said they were taken to the drunk tank. Looking down at my hands, he asked what I was doing down there so early.

"Dollarama?" he asked, confused by all the snacks.

I decided to be open with him about Damien. I'm not sure why. Mark was obviously special to me, and things were falling apart. I didn't ever expect to tell him how I felt, especially since he was dying. I just felt like I could confide in him about what was happening because we trusted each other.

"I'm headed to a hotel for the night. I have back-to-back shifts, and between you and me, Damien gets drunk and keeps me up a lot. He says a lot of nasty stuff to me and then says I just need to toughen up, but I can't get the words out of my head. They hurt."

"Well, of course, they do," he responded. "How long have you two been together?"

"Three and a half years," I replied.

"That's a long time," he said contemplatively.

We continued talking for a moment before he confirmed that I'd told him I was working that night, and we parted ways. It felt good to get that off my chest. I had a couple of long-distance friends who knew the situation in detail and my manager also knew the gist of it...but Mark was one of the first I was open with about it who lived here and didn't work with me.

As it would turn out, only three days later, Damien and I had another huge fight, and we broke up for good. He didn't leave the house for another month, but we were split. There was a sense of relief, but I wanted him out. He threatened to take my cat, Lumi, and all kinds of nonsense. He claimed he didn't mean it, but then why say it? Because he wanted to upset me. He'd often say he spent more time with her than I did (he was home all day because he was on the COVID benefit payments from the Federal Government). I had to work. I love my cat so much and he knew that and he had always said, "she's really your cat."

All spring, I'd been going out for walks to get away from him, and I continued to do this even after we split to try and avoid having to hear anything else hurtful. The relationship was long past expired, and I finally had the self-respect not to allow myself to be around that treatment anymore.

One day when I was off, I decided to walk back to my house from the Village Mall (at the west end of town). I was taking my time and talking to Jen on my cell, so it was over an hour that I was walking. As I made my way toward downtown, I honestly hoped Mark would be outside Marie's so I could see him, but he wasn't. I ran in to grab a cold bottle of water, talked to my manager for a bit, and then headed home.

The following day, Mark was in the store chatting with me while I was on my shift, and I was telling him about my walk the day before.

"Yeah, I know you were down here yesterday because we talked down that way," he motioned down the road. I can still picture him in my head now. We were near the entrance and he was back on to it while we were chatting

"We didn't talk yesterday," I responded, confused. "I didn't see you at all yesterday," I continued, causing him to look extremely confused himself.

Of course, I was *absolutely certain* I hadn't talked to him because I would have remembered that as I'd looked for him. I was hoping to just get to see him...even just briefly, let alone speak to him.

What was even weirder was that I had seen Mark in a dream before I woke up that morning. I couldn't recall ever dreaming of him before this. I knew we were talking in it, but I couldn't remember about what.

Now *how's that* for a bit of weirdness?

5 GUARDIAN ANGEL

Not much later, Mark, unfortunately, wound up in the hospital after throwing up blood. I'd been out for an evening walk a few days after this, still not wanting to go home right away because of Damien still being there. I ran into Mark and Jesse outside Subway, just across the street from Marie's, as someone handed them soup they'd bought for them. I stood there chatting with them about what was happening. Mark told me they had done an endoscopy and wanted him to stay to finish some fluids, but he wanted to leave. I told him he's not taking care of himself and that I'd clock him (jokingly) if he didn't start. He didn't look too well but was trying to eat anyhow.

Not long after this, I was working in the store when Mark came in looking for some milk. This was the second time he'd come in for milk that day. He informed me that there seemed to be no milk in the fridge, and apologized to me when I had to go in the back to get more. The milk in the back of the row had not slid to the front like it should and he couldn't reach it. I reassured him with a pat on the back that it was okay. He'd had a rough week. Getting milk was not exactly a huge chore. If I'm honest, I patted him on the back as an excuse to touch him. I had it *bad*.

"Can too much calcium hurt you?" he asked me.

"Yes," I responded, "but not just two small bottles like that."

His other bottle, almost empty from earlier, had a darker substance in it now. As he inserted his debit card into the machine, he told me he intended to make a White Russian.

"Mark, please don't," I responded.

"Okay, Mom... " he joked. That was one of his go-to sayings with people.

"Please, Mark, I care about you," I added as he punched in his PIN, telling him it had hit me hard that last time he ended up in the hospital.

"I know you care," he responded to my pleading with him.

“I want to keep seeing you smile for a long time yet,” I added.

“Smile? I have no teeth!” he laughed. He didn’t get how infectious his smile was with or without teeth. He continued, saying he was going to die alone in a hospital bed anyway and acted as if he had pretty much given up.

Some customers came in, so we couldn't continue the conversation. I watched helplessly as he went back outside, knowing what he was about to do to himself. I didn't talk to him again until the next day.

It was pouring rain when he and Jesse had come to sit outside the store, finding shelter under the roof. Mark came in looking for some milk and orange juice. I told him I was surprised to see him down there in the rain. I couldn’t recall seeing him sitting out in the rain much since I’d started working there the previous August.

"Gotta make the..." he cut himself off, rubbing his fingers together to imply money.

He said he was feeling a lot better because he got some alcohol into himself. His debit card wouldn’t work and he asked if he could borrow the milk and pay for that and the orange juice after. I said to not worry about it and I’d pay for it. He must have misunderstood since he ran down to his bank and came back later to pay me. I informed him again that I’d paid for it when he left earlier.

“I said I care and I mean it,” I told him, referring to the day before.

He stuck around and we got to talking more.

"What time are you off work?" he asked.

"Five. Mom's coming to pick me up, and then we're going to visit my grandma."

He told me more about his "grammy and grampy" and how much he loved them. I related to his feelings about his grandparents a lot.

"How old is she?" he asked.

"She'll be ninety in October."

“Ninety?” he said, sounding shocked.

"When I get to be Grandma's age, I want to be like Sophia on *The Golden Girls*. A smart-mouthed, little old lady,” I laughed as I told him.

"I'll be long gone," he responded with some sadness.

"Nope! No talking like that!" I tried to be positive for him. "You can beat this. You get sober, and you can get a new liver. I believe in you.”

When my shift ended about twenty minutes later, Mom was waiting in the car outside. When my co-worker showed up to take over the shift (it was a Friday, a two-shift day at the store), I gathered my change from tips and made my way out to the car. Mark was sitting closest to the door.

"So you guys get out of the rain quicker," I said, dropping the money in his cup.

“Have fun with Grammy,” he called out. He was sitting with Jesse and Suzie. This is not her real name but will be how I refer to her throughout the rest of the book. It’s inspired by someone’s nickname for her, but many also know her as “The Queen of Water Street.”

As I was about to get in the car, Jesse called out to me.

"Hey, Krista! What's your last name?"

"Murphy! Very Irish!" I joked as I got in the car. Newfoundland has a strong Irish heritage.

I sat down next to Mom and told her who they all were. When I got to Mark, my mom piped up.

"Oh, so that's Mark!"

I'd pointed him out months before when she'd picked me up. He'd been squeegeeing across the intersection. This was the closest she'd seen him at that point. I should have known she suspected something when she said that. I looked at Mark sitting with his legs crossed in front of him, looking down at his lap. For some reason, I got the feeling that sometimes when he came in the store, he wanted to ask me to hang out. Mom and I made our way to my grandmother’s, and little did I know what was about to happen that weekend.

I went in for my usual evening shift on Saturday and saw no sign of Mark and Jesse. This seemed odd to me; but I went about the evening, went home, and was about to go to bed when I saw my sister was trying to call me. I have a sister and two fraternal twin brothers through my dad. Knowing that I'd want to talk to her for more than five minutes, that it was late, and I'd have my Sunday morning shift the next day...I decided not to pick up. I'd call her back after my shift was done. A couple of minutes later, my phone rang again. This time it was my cousin.

"Ok, something's wrong," I thought.

When I picked up, she was upset and asked if I was sitting down.

"Well, I was about to go to sleep, so I'm lying down."

"Krista, I'm really sorry, but your dad had a heart attack tonight. He's gone."

I was stunned and couldn't believe what I was hearing. I felt I had to cut ties with my father in 2019 due to my inability to handle how he behaved (or didn't behave) with me. It wasn't our first estrangement over the years, starting with him not coming around enough in my early childhood. It was a complicated relationship ever since he left just before I turned two. It felt best just to discontinue it as he seemed like he would never completely act like a father to me. I felt like a side thought and that he didn't really care. It had always hurt me psychologically, and it was too hard to go through while also going through all the psychological damage I was dealing with from everything else.

I knew a heart attack or stroke was possible with my father as he was a massive man and loved his steaks and such. Dad was well known in the province and always on the news talking about gas prices as he was a taxi driver. He'd served the province for four years as an MHA before returning to dispatching during the last few years of his life, so I knew it would be all over the news. Talk about having a loss shoved in your face while you are grieving. It was inescapable. He passed away suddenly next to their fire pit in the backyard, something he loved to do.

My stepmother would later plant a tree with some of his ashes buried under it. After Mark passed away, she said I could also sprinkle some of his ashes around the tree, which I did. I really appreciated her offering that.

During the wake and funeral, a lot of information I'd previously not known came out. Many told me he spoke fondly of me, and I found out he had difficulty expressing love to the people closest to him. I think a lot of it is family pain passed down the line. My grandfather on that side of the family picked on Dad more than the other kids according to one of my uncles. There was a time or two that Dad made me feel the same way (intentionally or not). My grandfather had always been sweet to me, but we all know it's different between a father and a child. I sadly feel like I understand my father more in death than I did in life. I pray he has rest now. Everyone always felt I got my artistic ability from Dad, among other things.

Needless to say, I didn't go to work the next day. It was Sunday, and Mondays I always had off anyhow. Damien, still living at the house while trying to figure out where to go after our breakup, was compassionate toward me when I found this out. But the compassion was short-lived.

When I got to work on Tuesday, I saw Jesse and asked him where Mark was. He informed me that Mark had thrown up blood again on the weekend, and they had to call an ambulance. It was terrible...really bad. He said something about there being clots in the blood and everything. Between this and my father passing away, I had to lock the door for a short time after he left so I could go to the bathroom to cry. I couldn't leave the store unattended, but I needed to lock up as I knew I couldn't hold back the tears. It felt like life was falling apart around me.

When I came back out and unlocked the door, a couple of ladies from another nearby company came in and asked me if I wanted to interview for a job. Apparently, they thought I was a good worker. It was a job that I felt would be a good fit for my interests, so I decided to go for it as I thought it was right up my alley. It was the one bright spot for such a lousy week.

When I got home that day, Damien started bullying me again. Two days after my father had passed away and already having broken up...he still did it again. For me, this was atrocious and one of the most absurd and cruel things he'd done to me the whole time. Who does that? I became very confident in those moments that I'd made the right choice when we broke up in May. I went to stay with my mother and stepfather until after my father's funeral but had stopped into the apartment at least once during that time.

That Thursday, I was off work and went for another walk. It was a nice, sunny day, and I'd been thinking about everything...a lot. Having lost a couple of friends suddenly in the past and now my father, it was even more challenging for me knowing that Mark was sick. I had to get my feelings for him off my chest, but I didn't know if I wanted to tell him as I didn't know if he felt the same way (come to find out later, he more than felt the same way and had for a while). After visiting my apartment briefly, I decided to head downtown and went looking for Jesse. I wanted to discuss things with him and feel out the situation.

I left the house and made my way down to the area of Marie's. I cut down George Street, where most of the bars are, and heard *One Thing* by Finger Eleven playing. I remember the lyrics stood out to me and felt suiting. When I turned the corner, I saw Jesse and Suzie sitting together next to Mary Brown's Fried Chicken under the building's amazing mural. I often looked at it across the intersection through the window while at work. I sat down with them and found out how Mark was doing.

When Jesse had seen him, he said he was in so much pain he was rolling back and forth in his hospital bed. We talked about Damien and me, and I confided in them about how he had been treating me. In hindsight, I'd imagine Mark may have already told Jesse some of it. They said while an asshole can be an alcoholic, alcoholics are not always assholes. Obviously!

"Be careful; that's that mind-bending shit," Jesse responded.

He and Suzie both told me it's one thing to be an alcoholic, but it's another to be cruel. Suzie told me she felt I was a very smart girl and didn't deserve that kind of treatment. She has a lot more wisdom than some give her credit for. She doesn't just suffer from alcoholism, but also has a brain injury and used to have a great job. She has a good heart and means well. I've learned a lot through talking to people who hang out downtown, and not just from Mark. As I've said, everyone has a story.

After a while, I felt comfortable enough to address what I wanted to say. At this point, Suzie was doing her own thing, so I summoned the courage to bring things up.

"Can you keep a secret?"

"Depends on what it is," Jesse replied, informing me if it's something serious and bad he'd not be able to.

I told him it wasn't anything like that. I then told him I'd had feelings for Mark for a while, but didn't know if I wanted to tell him. I wanted to get it off my chest, only I didn't think Mark felt the same. We had a brief chat about it.

"I know you said you don't want to tell him...but if he's dying, can I tell him and watch his heart rate spike on the monitor?"

We both laughed.

"Yeah, sure," I said. Though in my mind, I was asking myself, "Why does he think Mark's heart rate will spike?"

"Neither of us sleep very well. I think if he knew, he'd sleep better than he has in a long time," he added.

"What does he know that I don't?" I started asking myself.

The next day I was working at Queen's Road Store (also owned by Marie's), and Jesse popped in. That's when I told him I felt I would tell Mark about my feelings at some point soon. He had his bandana over the bottom of his face because of COVID, but I could tell he was smiling because of his eyes. When I told him I'd decided to tell Mark how I felt, he clasped his hands over his heart in the goofiest way.

"My heart!" he said happily. He told me he felt like Mark could make it.

So, we made plans that I'd head up to St. Clare's with him one day soon when he went to see Mark again (and he knew he was feeling at least somewhat okay). We discussed how tough Mark was and how he was like the Keith Richards of St. John's. Because, like Keith, he'd probably outlive the cockroaches if there was a nuclear war. If only that had been true. As of that point, Jesse told me he hadn't told Mark anything I'd said the day before.

After my father's funeral, I returned to my apartment. Damien was still there, and the reality of the breakup had hit him while I'd been gone. When I got home, he was emotional and admitted he'd blown it. I reminded him that I had told him for a long time that if something didn't change, he would kill our relationship. He asked if there was any hope at all, and I told him no. I wasn't sure why it was coming as such a shock to him. We'd been broken up for a couple of weeks at that point, but I guess he just thought it would blow over, and it didn't. Even during this conversation, though he kept trying to apologize, I could tell he didn't mean it.

"Well, look at this as a wake-up call to turn your life around," I told him. "I have an interview tomorrow for another job. I was approached about it because they saw me at work and thought I was good."

"Nice tits," he responded.

"No! It was two women! Really? Nice tits? That's the only thing you think is going to get me another job?" I responded (though in hindsight, it obviously doesn't matter that it was women). Either way, he was very wrong.

"You're a hard worker; I take it back."

This is how all "apologies" went with him.

During the next few days, I'd go out on my walks and run into Jesse, so he'd go for a stroll with me. When we would hang out we'd talk about Mark and various things, including his own life. He told me about his best friend, Yvonne, and how she was into art like me.

One day I told him my nickname with my family as a child was "Kissy" (like Krissy without the r). Well, I regretted that very quickly when Jesse wandered into the store a couple of days later. I waved at him when he entered, and with a mischievous grin he says, "Hey Kissy." Never tell anyone embarrassing childhood nicknames! Well, now you all know too!

Another day, Jesse returned from the hospital and told me that Mark was well enough to eat and go out for a smoke.

"I didn't tell him what you told me, but..." I honestly wondered if he'd embarrassed me. He'd decided to let him know about how I'd said that I missed him and couldn't wait to see him again. I *had* told him to tell him *that part*. "I think she likes you a lot," he told me he'd added.

"No way! That's awesome!" Mark responded with the biggest grin, Jesse said. He said it looked like it gave him butterflies in his stomach.

When we finally went to see him, he was on the seventh floor of the hospital, lying on his bed in his overalls. He was looking pretty well, considering what he'd been through, though he was a little frailer looking. He lifted his pants to show us how his leg was swollen from water. The same had happened to his left hand. We chatted, and he wanted to run downstairs in his wheelchair for a smoke. So, we got his coat on and wheeled him out front. Another man who frequented downtown, whose name escapes me, had been in there for foot surgery and came over to chat with us as well. It came up about my father passing away, and the man told me how he'd met my father a few times and said he always gave him money and spoke to him. Jesse and I were sitting on the ground...actually, at this point, he was lying on the ground against the hospital wall. The rest of us continued chatting.

Mark spoke up at one point and said he'd had a better sleep the night before than he had in a long time. I thought back to what Jesse had said before, about how if Mark knew how I felt, he'd probably sleep better. After learning he'd somewhat spilled the beans the day before, I found it ironic that Mark had said this.

Damien came up at one point, and Mark was asking me if he'd moved out yet. I said no, but that he was in the process and how I couldn't wait until I had freedom and not be scared to be in my own home for fear of getting badgered. I can't recall exactly what I said, but Mark, still in his wheelchair having a smoke, stared toward the distance. He began calling Damien a few different expletives I can't recall exactly word for word now. You could see how pissed off it had made him that I was put through the mental abuse I had dealt with, and he only knew such a small amount compared to what had happened. Unless, maybe, Jesse had told him some of the stuff we'd chatted about while walking around.

As we all sat there talking, Jesse became more and more sleepy. He was also more than a little drunk. He wanted to get down to The Gathering Place (a shelter here in the city), but didn't have money for a cab. I didn't want to have to leave yet. I wanted to talk to Mark. I told Jesse not to worry about it, ran inside to the ATM to grab him a twenty, and he was on his way.

Eventually, it was just me and Mark left, and I wheeled him back up to his room with a million thoughts going through my head. I was so nervous. I keep telling everyone now that I wouldn't have been nervous if I had known then what I found out from everyone later.

We got to Mark's room and he got out of his chair to sit on the bed. He said something along the lines of "Well, I guess you better be going, darlin'." I had never heard him use that word before. It was cute.

"Actually, could I talk to you about something?" I asked. He said sure, and I found myself unable to get the words out. "So..." I took a deep breath and paused. "I really don't know how to say this." It took a few seconds, but I finally spoke again. "I'm just going to spit it out. I like you!" He could tell from my hesitancy and inability to find the right words that I was nervous. I told him how complicated my life had been, but that I knew there had been something that I couldn't, or wouldn't, label for months. I told him I'd essentially had a crush on him.

"Well, if it means anything, just so you know, I think you're awesome too," he responded somewhat sheepishly. A wave of relief came over me. "Maybe when I get out of here, we can go catch a flick. We can shoot popcorn at people." He insisted he wanted to pay for it. I laughed at the thought of throwing popcorn and agreed, saying that would be fun. "And who knows? Maybe you're like my..." He paused like he was trying to think of the word or phrase. "It's on the tip of my tongue," but he couldn't recall. Then he blurted out, "Guardian angel." He said that it wasn't exactly the proper term, but he "couldn't think of it." It was ironic because I'd viewed him as one of mine, sitting outside the store while I was working.

He informed me he would be in there a bit longer as they were giving him a liver stent. He'd already had a different procedure to help some of the bleeding varices in his esophagus. Varices are enlarged veins that can form with liver disease because of obstructed blood flow in the portal vein. It carries blood from your digestive tract, gallbladder, etc. The stent was to help relieve the pressure of the blood going through the liver where it was damaged and didn't function right.

We talked for a bit, and after the nurse came in to take his blood pressure and give him his pills, I decided to head out. I hugged him and headed home, relieved that I'd finally gotten my feelings off my chest. When I got home, I called my friend Jen about everything.

"You are too cute. I love that when you talk about him it reminds me of two teens having girls' night talking about boys," she responded.

Jesse had woken up at The Gathering Place that night and shot me a quick message around 3 am.

“I just woke up. Mark messaged me. He seemed happy you told him.”

The next evening, I went to stay with my mother for another couple of days to get some peace after Damien had started up with me again. At least I was closer to the hospital then.

Mark was hospitalized for about another week after they gave him the liver stent. When I went to see him after it was done, he had a tube down his throat and couldn't speak or move, though he looked at me. I remember telling him I'd hug him, but I was scared I'd pull something out. There were so many wires and such. He shifted his body in the bed slightly to face me when I said this, and he was staring me in the eyes. I wondered if he was saying to do it anyhow, but I didn't risk it. We just stared at each other for a bit, it was probably only ten to twenty seconds, but it felt like longer. It was long enough that it felt like it meant more, and I felt slightly awkward wondering what he was thinking (if anything). He was probably pretty drugged up either way and I'd be surprised if he even remembered it later.

In the days following, he was slightly delirious in the ICU and going out of his skin feeling like he needed alcohol. He had difficulty speaking the day after the tube came out, and I remember him crying and a tear rolling down the side of his face. He was going through a lot. When he was finally able to speak again, his voice had been messed up (from the tube, I suppose), and he never quite sounded exactly like himself again. He was very raspy and sounded more aged. He was also cranky that a male nurse had shaved his face.

"I don't feel like I look like me when my face is shaved. He just went and did it when I was knocked out."

We had a few laughs even during the misery of him being stuck in the ICU. He got a kick out of my impression of Harry, another much older panhandler from downtown. I often saw Harry on my morning walks to work, and we'd say hello. I just found out this past March that he had passed away over the winter. The poor man was found frozen to death on the street. He'd often come into the store and was always very friendly with me, but like so many, he had a big problem with alcohol. He'd dig into his pockets looking for money after asking for his beer.

“Let's see if I have enough...Oooooh!” he'd exclaim with surprise as he took out a wad of bills, laughing.

I still wonder whether he already knew he had enough or if he was just joking with me. Mark cracked up at my goofy impression of him and thought it was just like him. It was nice to make him laugh like that, but he had a bad feeling that he would drink again when he got out.

"Hang out with me!" I suggested happily.

"Definitely," he replied.

He did drink when he got out but not nearly as heavy as he usually would have. I hugged him before leaving one day, and he kissed my neck as I was bent over him. I said when he got out, that I would give him a real kiss.

"I might get off thinking about that," he joked as I left.

He called me on Facebook one morning within the week (he had a cell but no monthly phone plan). I'd still been working at Marie's, but I was trying out the new job on my days off. He'd asked me if I wanted company on my walk to work. I tried to tell him it wasn't a good idea, but didn't argue much as I knew he was stubborn. He said he'd see me at the store; so when I got there Jesse was sitting outside and I told him Mark was planning to leave. He immediately got a cab to the hospital to stop him. He ended up banned for a time because they saw he had a bottle of alcohol in his jacket and felt he was going to give it to Mark. No one was allowed to visit for the rest of the day because of it, but at least Mark ended up staying.

He called me again the next day, but this time I'd missed it. I tried calling the nursing station, and they said he'd already left. He was not in a state yet to be leaving so soon. Worried, I found Jesse again, and we searched everywhere for him but couldn't find him.

6 INTERTWINED

After a mad dash trying to figure out where Mark went, Jesse and I eventually parted ways. The following day, I walked to Marie's to open, and who should be sitting out front but Jesse and Mark. Jesse had found him at The Gathering Place after we gave up looking the evening before. Mark's apartment had damage caused by all the blood he'd vomited the last time he wound up in the hospital. No one knew it was there for half that time, and it had started to rot at the floor, so they were getting it repaired. So, they slept there (though Mark disliked this immensely) and made their way down to the store in the morning. He was pale and didn't look well. His left hand was even more messed up than it was before. We figured it was something to do with the IV damaging something.

I gave him a hug and the kiss I promised before I opened. I took a few pictures of him and Jesse and went to work. A little while later, Mark wandered into the store after I'd opened. He came in looking almost like a bashful teenage boy and said that when he got his cheque, he wanted to take me to that movie and for me to pick out one I'd like to go to. I can still remember hugging him while he was in the store and remembering how many times I'd wished I could do that when he came in before his hospital stay. There weren't many good movie choices at the time, but I picked one. We never went afterwards, as he felt too sick and the movie choices were terrible anyhow.

Instead of returning to The Gathering Place, I invited them to stay with me. Damien and I had agreed that he would no longer be at the apartment when I was there. Then at the end of the month, he would get me to taxi his things to his new location since they would all fit in a van. So, there were no worries of a run-in happening. I'm unsure how Mark would have handled that, as he seemed pretty upset at what had been said to me. It didn't matter for very long, as the day came to send Damien's stuff over in a taxi, and all was over. I've tried being friendly with him when he'd message me later, and it always turned into more immaturity and invalidation on his part. So, keeping my distance was best, and I blocked his messages.

When the guys came to the house, it didn't take very long before Mark noticed something amongst the mess on the table that I still had at that time.

"That's a cool picture," he commented.

The image was of a large sailing ship on a calm sea, with Christ and the dove representing the Holy Spirit, in the sky above watching over it. The whole picture was monochromatic in shades of blue. At the time it surprised me that he took note of that, of all things, but not so much in hindsight with what I came to find out. With Damien being moved out, I was doing an overhaul of some possessions. Some I was getting rid of, and some were pictures I had yet to hang. I wasn't a Christian at the time, but I still had an appreciation for my upbringing. The picture he noticed used to belong to my grandfather and it had hung on the wall throughout my childhood.

During this time, I also got to know Jesse's friend Yvonne (whom he had told me about), by chatting with her over the phone. She was supposed to come to Newfoundland a few weeks later to be with Jesse during Mark's illness. We got along very well, and I was looking forward to meeting her in person and possibly doing artwork together.

Mark had commented on a painting on the wall that I did of a girl crying surrounded by faces. It was inspired by the mental abuse I'd dealt with. It also reminded me of when I was bullied in school. I'd hear the unkind words said over and over in my head, and it felt like they taunted me.

I feel Mark understood it.

It felt very natural for all of us to be together from the moment they came to stay at the house, and the same can be said for when Yvonne would arrive later. The four of us would become like a little family.

The moment Mark was out of the hospital and at my house (and we could see each other in private), it was like we had been together forever. He was cuddling into me on the couch right away.

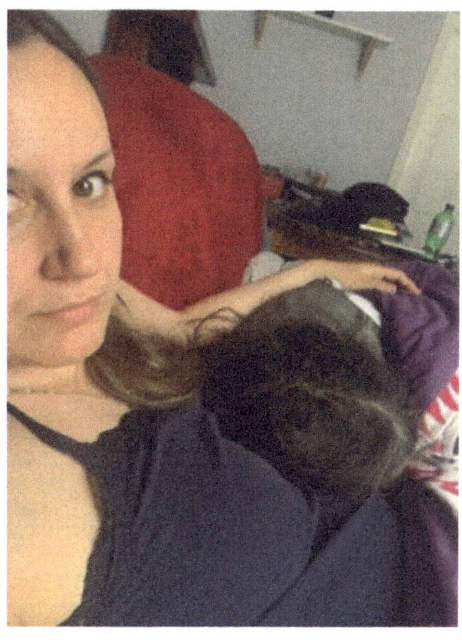

"It's been forever since I cuddled with a woman like this. It's almost better than sex," he joked.

Not that he didn't cop a feel. He conveniently had his hand under his head at one point (which was lying on my chest), and of course, the fingers started squeezing slightly.

Smooth. Real smooth.

I didn't mind. We seemed to have this understanding between us from the very beginning. We were nuts about each other.

One day, Jesse went to pick up more alcohol while Mark and I had a cuddle session on the couch again as we watched TV. I was cuddled in under his arm with mine wrapped around his torso. He was slowly and lovingly stroking my hair and face as his hand shook from the withdrawal. His breathing deepened a bit as he did it. There was something so sad and tender about him as he was doing this, it was almost poetic.

We had a lot of conversations those first couple of days...deep conversations. He told me some very personal stuff that had happened to him when he was younger and experiences that he'd had with strangers that were not easy to hear about. He asked me at one point what my opinion on marriage was. I wasn't sure what to tell him as I wasn't expecting him to ask me that.

Number one: I'd been married twice, and it never went well. But on the other hand, if the right person came along and I *truly* felt they were honest (unlike the other two), I wasn't against it. If I was going to do it, I wanted to be sure. I honestly didn't think he would be interested in marriage. So, I just told him I didn't believe you needed a piece of paper because you will either work out or not, regardless...but I wasn't against it either. I regret addressing his question this way deeply now. I wish I'd been completely honest. He said he agreed that you don't need a piece of paper to prove you love someone. We both considered it true, but I would find out information from our friend Barry later that clarified this conversation much more for me.

Mark also asked me if I had any kids. I told him, no, but in 2009 I had suspected a possible miscarriage as I'd been bleeding for seventeen days, and it had not started when I was due for my cycle. There was also the possibility that it could have also been an ovarian cyst. At the time, I was (for whatever reason) scared to go to a doctor and find out. He brought up how his ex-girlfriend had aborted the twins when he was eighteen. He'd told me about the twins before but stated how they'd have been about twenty-two years old...not far off from Jesse's age. I think that deep down, it may have bothered him that they'd been aborted, as he had brought them up more than once. We touched on a lot of personal topics in a very short amount of time and opened up to each other very naturally. We spewed it all out as if we'd already known each other for years.

Neither of us had human children, but we'd both been parents to fur babies—me with my cat, Lumi, of course. Mark used to have a dog named Maggo (pronounced Magoo...like *Mr. Magoo*) that he loved so much and had picked her out as a puppy. The cops had taken her from him when he had been arrested once and brought her to a pound instead of letting him bring her to his friend's house nearby. He told me a bit about her and still seemed upset about it to that day. I understand that...don't mess with someone and their fur babies. I'd be heartbroken about that too and would have always wondered about them.

We often all took turns putting songs on YouTube and played a lot of metal. Mark loved Manowar, and I'd been introduced to them by my ex-husband. I also introduced him to Nightwish as he said he wasn't familiar with them. I find that hard to believe, so maybe he just forgot. Both Mark and Jesse also liked Johnny Cash, just like I do. I remember one of us (who knows now which one of us) put on the song *Hurt*. It was Johnny's cover of the Nine Inch Nails song and is a long-time favourite of mine, and the video is amazing.

"I wanna meet Johnny and June when I die," Mark spoke up.

A man after my own heart, as I want to meet them too. I thought it was cute he wanted to meet Johnny *and* June. I had hoped he wouldn't meet them for a long time, considering they were long passed away.

I told him how I'd made a bunch of YouTube videos in the past. One was a dedication to Jim Henson with clips from *The Muppet Show, Sesame Street*, and *Fraggle Rock*, and he enthusiastically declared how much he loved *Sesame Street*, but hadn't seen it in ages. I told him how I had a DVD of *Christmas Eve on Sesame Street*, which was a TV special from the eighties I'd seen as a child.

"No way! We need to watch that together on Christmas Eve!"

He couldn't have gotten any cuter than he was by saying this. Who'd have thought? This is the side of him that many didn't get to see. He was tough, but he was also so sweet and such a teddy bear.

The first make out session was pretty funny. Jesse was asleep on the floor, and we were both on my couch as we were watching *Shameless*. Anyhow, he grabbed me and started to immediately French kiss me.

"There's only so much I can take," he commented as we pulled away from each other momentarily, before kissing me again.

He found it a special kind of torture to sit with me watching TV, Jesse asleep on the floor, and not just go for it.

Jesse often fell asleep on the floor with Mark and me hogging my small couch. Jesse's brother Justin messaged me on Facebook at one point, asking if he was okay. He knew that the last time they'd spoken over my phone, Jesse said his phone had been stolen. Justin hadn't heard from him for a while, so we took a goofy video of Mark teasing Jesse.

"Wakey, wakey!" he said as he shook Jesse with his foot. "Safe and sound, Justin!"

Jesse was out cold.

"He sounds different," he replied with shock at the state of Mark's voice on the video.

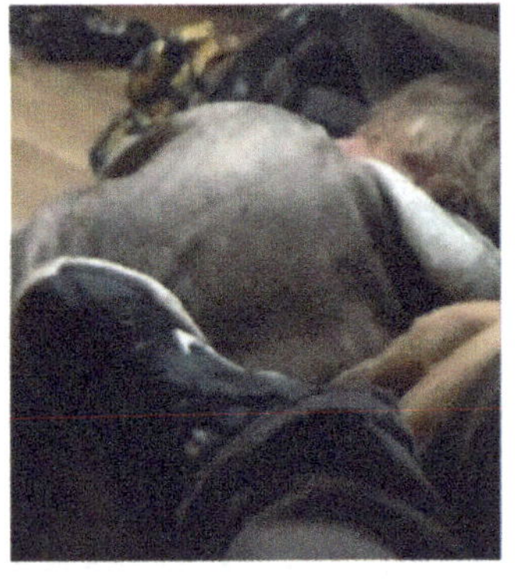

Jesse had initially met Mark a few years before as his brother had known him first (while on the street), and he had recommended that Jesse get to know him when he visited.

"Praise Jesus!" Mark told me to type playfully. It wasn't at all mocking; he was just being silly. He knew Justin had turned to Christ in recent years.

We did talk a little bit about spiritual stuff at this point. At one point we were talking about paranormal experiences and I couldn't help but ask him something.

"If you do end up passing away...will you come back to see me if it's possible, and make yourself known?"

This was coming from a place of fear. There was nothing I wanted more than for him to stay alive, but I knew he was very sick.

"Of course I will," he responded.

When I got home from work that Saturday night, Mark was asleep on my couch, and Jesse was on the floor a short bit away from him. I decided to try not to wake them up. I felt gross after my shift and went to have a shower. I threw on a tight black camisole and some navy-blue drawstring pants and went into the bedroom to comb and dry my hair.

I heard a little coughing and talking coming from the living room (which was still dark). I got up while brushing my wet hair and stood, a shadowy figure in the doorway, asking Mark what he was saying. He'd been talking while half asleep. As soon as he saw me, he immediately started trying to slap Jesse (who was still out) on the shoulder very enthusiastically.

"*Holy fuck*, Jesse! Krista's *ready* for me! Look!" he said as he continued to slap at Jesse's shoulder awkwardly from the couch.

I started laughing hysterically. He was still half asleep, but began to wake up more. He came into the bedroom with me after I was done drying my hair and asked me what he'd said while groggy on the couch because he couldn't remember. He lost it laughing when I told him, and was maybe also a little embarrassed. Mark slept in my bed with me, but contrary to his reputation, he held back from anything more.

"I really want to fuck you, but...I still don't have any energy. People would be confused that I haven't jumped you yet. I even told my social worker, Amy, about you. I told her this feels like my last chance to have a normal relationship. And it's frustrating because my hand doesn't even work. I have always been so independent, but I feel like an old man needing help all the time."

He went on to say that he and Jesse had talked about us, and Jesse suggested that he shouldn't rush it with me anyhow. That way, I'd understand it was about more than just sex with me. So, he kissed my breast and laid his head on my chest. We were cuddling in bed and facing each other with legs completely intertwined while we just talked. He ran his hand all over my back, under my shirt. He'd slid his hand slightly down the back of my pants, played with the top of my underwear, and pulled his hand out after a minute or so.

"I have to stop; this is gonna kill me," he said. "Man, I hate it when you like...love someone...and you're up late...like...getting to know them...*hint hint*...and you mean to sleep, but you can't stop talking."

Love someone, eh? I didn't take it too seriously at the time, as I didn't know what I know now.

He confided in me one night about how he'd been on the streets and living that life for so long, that it might be hard for him to get away from it completely. But then he continued saying that he felt like he might want to learn a trade someday. He'd also said that he thought a lot about if he were to get completely sober. He was still drinking some White Russian every day to try and keep from withdrawing...but was definitely not drunk. He felt that if he could somehow get sober and receive a liver transplant, he'd even like to possibly learn someday how to become a trucker. This is something he talked about in his writing as well. He said he loved the idea of speeding down a highway in a large truck while blasting music, no doubt something like Iron Maiden or Mötley Crüe. I can picture him now driving down the highway, belting out *Kickstart My Heart*...but who knows, maybe it would end up being the Cranberries. He admitted he had a soft spot for them—especially their song *Linger*. I don't think I know anyone who doesn't like that song—what a big softy. But rightfully so...they're awesome. I told him to focus on getting well before coming up with job ideas, but it was great he was thinking about long-term goals. This was much different than when he'd been talking to me in the store about dying in a hospital bed.

He asked me if I'd ever attempted suicide before. We'd just watched *What Dreams May Come* on Jesse's suggestion, and Robin William's wife in the film kills herself (not to mention what happened to poor Robin in real life). I told him I hadn't attempted it, but seriously considered it at a few very low points in my life. I usually contemplated walking into traffic. He revealed to me he'd attempted suicide a few times in his life, including in the bathroom of a bar on George Street.

"Of all places," he said.

In the movie, Robin's character is angry with Cuba Gooding Jr. at his suggestion that his wife is lost for eternity in hell. He indignantly fights back, saying he's her soulmate and will save her.

"YEAH!" Mark cheered in a gruff voice. It made me smile. It was beautiful. The man was a hopeless romantic, whether he openly admitted to it or not.

Jesse used the term soulmates on Mark and me often. The first time he said it to me was when I told him I didn't understand how I could be around Mark even when he was vomiting, as I had always been very phobic before then.

"Soulmates," he'd respond with an impish grin.

He's told me recently (as of writing this) that he wouldn't use that term lightly. He'd forgotten he'd used it to describe us but said he still agreed with the assessment. People can delude themselves into thinking someone is their soulmate. For varying immature reasons, I did it on more than one occasion over the course of my life. With Mark and I, it was apparent to those who saw us together or heard us talk about each other. I put no label on us while living out the relationship, as I just wanted to experience it and love him. Our relationship was based on nothing but love and no delusions. But if there's anything to the idea in any form...I agree with Jesse. We were a unique and special pair, and his assessment was correct.

When it came to bedtime, other than being affectionate, we joked around a lot.

"I wouldn't put my head under the covers if I were you," he said after he farted one night.

I told him I could tell he farted because I could feel him push, and we had such a laugh over that. He was cold, and we were completely intertwined (as usual), so it was easy to feel those little things. We calmed down, and I could feel his chest spasming again after a few seconds because I was lying on it.

He was trying to hold back his laughter. So, naturally, I made a fart noise with my mouth, knowing it would cause him to crack—no pun intended on the word usage. Well, we both burst into laughter...again.

"Do girls even fart?" he asked, laughing still. "They're always *so* embarrassed."

I told him we do, but that we're told that it's not ladylike.

"I'd fart right now, but I don't have one in me," I added.

It was such a childish conversation, but we had so many laughs. Jesse was in the living room and probably thought we were fooling around or something. No, no. We were just laughing at toilet humour like a couple of children. Oh my!

We also had some deep conversations about my last relationship. I told him how both Damien and my ex-husband had said no one would want me after two failed marriages, and it pissed him off.

"That's *bullshit*! You're hot as fuck, and beautiful in there," he said as he tapped on my lower chest.

This meant so much more to me than he probably even realized at the time. My self-esteem was absolutely destroyed, but it meant so much to me that he didn't believe all that stuff to be true himself. He was already showing me unconditional, non-judgmental love, and it still makes me well up with tears thinking about it.

During this time, the guys got up a couple of times to walk to work with me so they could go panhandle outside the store. I was still working at Marie's and working at the other business on my days off.

I won't lie...I was exhausted. Mark was too, though for different reasons. He didn't typically stick around as long anymore as he'd easily get tired. One day he came into the store and wanted to give me a five-dollar bill before returning to my house.

"What's that for?"

"For you to get a cab home after work," he replied. The store was about a fifteen-minute walk or a very short car ride.

"You keep that! I don't need that. I always walk when it's a nice day like today...but thank you."

"Are you sure?"

"Yes," I responded. This was the sweetest gesture considering Mark had so much less than me. People can take these kinds of gestures for granted.

One day he got my keys off me. I can't recall now where Jesse was this day, but he wasn't with Mark. He'd only had a few beers to try and not get sick and packed everything into his bag to head back to my apartment to rest.

I called him a cab, and when it arrived, I watched them talk for a minute. I asked myself if Mark had gotten confused about the address, as that happened sometimes. I'd find out why later. The cab finally took off. I had told him to make sure that if he did go out again, to be in the house at the time I'd be getting home from work. I had to be able to get in since he had my keys. At one point I tried calling my landline to make sure he had arrived, but there was no answer. He hadn't had his cell phone ever since he and Jesse had stayed at The Gathering Place. He'd left his backpack there, including his cell phone, and only brought a few things initially to my apartment.

They hadn't known I was going to offer for them to stay with me. At the time, Mark had assumed they'd return to the shelter and didn't bring his bag down to the store that morning, so I obviously couldn't call that.

I'd assumed he'd fallen asleep, as he was often groggy these days. I nervously approached the house, but there was no answer when I knocked on my windows. I went to my upstairs neighbour and asked her if I could come in through our shared laundry room. We jimmied the door from the laundry room to my kitchen, and I saw no sign of Mark whatsoever.

Confused, I got changed and headed back out with my extra keys to try and find him or see if I would run into Jesse, which I did. Then we both tried looking around for him together (again) and couldn't find him.

Eventually, a cop car pulled into the parking lot of the Supreme Court as we walked by. This is where the drunk tank is, so Jesse told me to wait a second. When the cop stepped out, he asked if Mark was in the drunk tank, and was told yes. The cop had Mark's coat and bag and was bringing them inside. He said they'd found him wandering and confused in an area just past where I was living. Jesse reassured me that Mark would be out early in the morning. I said it didn't make sense because he'd only had a couple of beers and was very much sober when he left work. It was all about to make sense the following morning. He wasn't drunk, but he was delirious. He needed a hospital, not the drunk tank.

7 | I LOVE YOU, TOO

Stressed out, I returned home alone. I called up Jen as usual and chatted with her for a bit, and tried to sleep eventually. I had a meeting at the new workplace early the next morning and afterwards I'd be going to Marie's to open for my usual shift. I had a hard time sleeping and fell asleep on my couch. I had only been asleep for two hours or so when a knock came on my living room window. It was Jesse, at about half past five in the morning.

He asked if he could crash at my place, and though I was frustrated, I said okay. I informed him I'd had difficulty sleeping and couldn't talk. I wanted to stay on the couch, so he took his usual spot on the floor. I reminded him to go straight to sleep, but he did get talkative as he was a little plastered. He asked if he could put some music on YouTube on my Roku. I said yes, but told him again that he had to stop talking. He didn't. I laugh about it now, but at the time I was frustrated. I went into my room, closed the door, and went back to sleep. Bless his heart, it's not like he was being mean.

When I got up and got ready for my meeting, I couldn't wake him up. He was lying on my small couch that was much too small to fit his height, so his legs were hanging off the arm of the chair slightly. I kept trying to wake him to no avail. So, what did I do? I grabbed him and pulled him off the couch. He hit the floor with a thud and still didn't wake up; he just laid there like a lump, if you can imagine. He was breathing, so I knew he was okay. Though in hindsight, that feels silly. Oh, he's not dead; he's fine! He's still breathing. Right, Krista. Right. Continuing to try and wake him up, I began to drag him across the smooth floor, and by the time we reached the kitty litter box clear across the living room, he finally started to stir, almost plopping into it.

I told him he had to hurry up because I had to leave, and I knew he wouldn't want to be in the house all day. I managed to get him out the door, but he had to sit outside for a moment.

"I'm sorry, but I have to boot it, or I'll be late," I told him as I left the poor kid sitting alone on the sidewalk. To this day, Jesse is like a little brother to me, and I think this was the moment it really started to feel that way.

I went to the morning meeting, and when it was over, we had to do a fire drill so that everyone knew where all the exits were in the event of a fire. When we came out of the meeting room, Jesse was sitting in a chair and told my new boss he had to talk to me about something important. She informed him I'd be available to talk soon, so he went back outside. She knew all the panhandlers herself. The fire drill took us outside, and as we walked back to the main entrance, I saw Mark sitting with Jesse in front of Marie's.

When I came back out, they weren't there anymore. I went into Marie's and got my uniform on to prepare for my shift and came outside again after everything was ready. Mark was getting assistance walking up onto the curb and it was almost like watching a baby learning to walk. I'll never forget those big blue eyes looking up at me and him being so frail as he walked in my direction. I can still see him in my head. He wasn't well, and he wasn't completely making sense when he spoke. Everyone wanted to call an ambulance for him, but he didn't want one. He was delirious and had lost his bag, his vest that we all knew so well, and his wallet. The wallet was found afterwards, but the vest and hat he'd had were long gone. To this day, I still wish I had that vest. I saw him in it so often while I was working at Marie's.

He'd not been drunk at all the night before. He'd been sick, but because of his reputation and the fact that he had some beers in his bag, I suppose the police had assumed that he was wandering drunk. It wouldn't have been a stretch considering his past.

He sat on the stoop in front of Marie's. I sat down next to him in my uniform, putting my arms around him and giving him pecks on the cheek.

I asked him if he would agree to go in an ambulance, and he said no. I asked him if he'd do it for me...and he got quiet. Ah! I got him with that one!

"I'm going to call," I said as I whipped out my cell phone.

He wasn't happy about it, but he agreed to do it. When the paramedics arrived, they asked him what year it was, and he said some year in the 1800s. They got him onto a stretcher, and we all stood at the opening of the ambulance and waved as they loaded him in. I blew him kisses, and he was off to get the help he needed. The ambulance would be called many times that summer, but not once was I ever allowed to go with him. I always had to go on my own because of COVID restrictions. He didn't seem to be in immediate danger, so I went inside and got to work. I brought his coat inside, put it away with my things, and went about my shift worried the whole day.

On and off throughout the day, various locals, from restaurant managers to the construction workers from the site next door, came in asking me how "my man" was doing. Word travelled fast. Even people who hadn't been there in the morning asked me about us later. It was madness. Downtown St. John's!

When my shift was finished, I went outside where our friend Barry was sitting and panhandling.

"I heard you helped Mark get in the ambulance. I love Mark. Thank you." He seemed a little emotional.

He started to confide in me that he'd estimated maybe five months or so before Mark had told him that he loved me and said if he were to get married, he'd marry me. Barry had tears in his eyes, and I knew he was being sincere. It blew my mind that over the months I had pined for him, he was pining for me too.

"You know what he said to me?" he said, suddenly turning to me. "He said that he'd give up drinking for you."

He said Mark had dozens of "girlfriends" before, but he'd never heard him say once that he *loved* any of them.

"*But he said he loved you.*" He said this with a pensive look on his face, his eyes completely glassy with tears. Barry was *very* emotional talking about this, and he had me crying at this point. I sat there next to him, hugging Mark's coat. He swore there was way more to Mark's feelings than just sex.

Because he had mentioned the dozens of "girlfriends," I asked him if Mark was definitely a one-woman man. Mark had told me it wasn't just about sex, but I wanted to see what Barry would say. If all he wanted was sex, Barry said Mark had *plenty* of women who would be willing to do it.

"I hear he's well hung, too!" he joked, nudging me and laughing.

I asked him if he was absolutely sure Mark had said "love" and not "like."

"Oh no, this was *way more* than like." he said. "He didn't know how to talk to you. He didn't know what to say."

Another time we talked, he swore that if Mark survived the cirrhosis, his next tattoo would say, "Krista."

"No, it won't; come on now," I laughed at him saying such a thing. I found it hard to believe with my self-esteem still in ruins from my previous relationship.

"No, *really*, have you seen all his tattoos?"

He was dead serious.

I want to add that I have spent quite a bit of time sitting outside with my friends that I met at Marie's and through Mark, and I'm not too fond of the way many people react to them. Some will stop and ask how they wound up in their situation, and it's fine. I know there will always be bad apples in any group of people...and I've met them too...but many of them are very nice people. I've watched as people walked by and ignored them completely. At least acknowledge them...they're human too! I've had people look at me, assuming I'm a panhandler when I've sat out there. They shoot me with "a look." Well, surprise! I don't panhandle. But I did, and still do, love someone who did. I have no regrets about that.

I made my way up to St. Clare's to see Mark and he was not doing well. He couldn't keep warm, and he kept throwing up. As I've said, I had been phobic of throwing up for a long time due to my experiences with severe illness and the fact that it nearly killed me. But overall, with Mark, I was able to handle it somehow by the grace of God. Somehow, I was able to deal with being around it with him. I was told on that first day that they were doing a blood culture to see if he had an infection of some kind. He started to come around with antibiotics over the next few days, and when I asked the nurse what the problem had been, she told me it was "gram-positive cocci."

One day when I arrived, I pulled the chair up to the head of the bed. He was lying against the railing with his pillow, so I was looking down at the top of his head and nose. He slowly turned his head up toward me with those bright blue eyes and simply said, “Hi Krista,” in this too-cute-to-not-be-intentional tone. Did he know he could melt my heart with those eyes? I don’t know, but it worked.

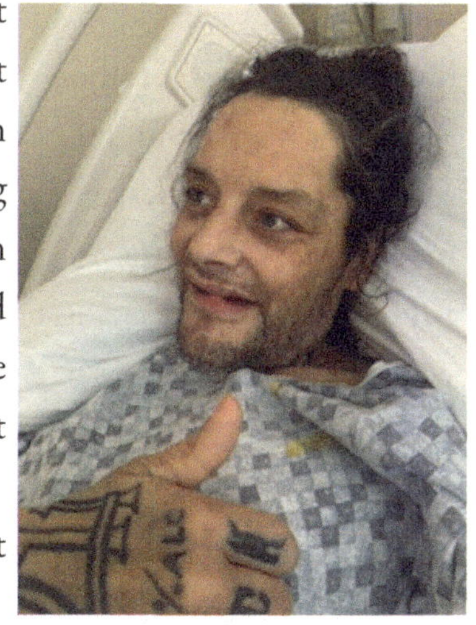

He was on the mend, so I made a point to tease him now about the man bun that the hospital had given him since he’d been in there (playfully). I told him how I was moving on to my new job for sure after the test run I'd had. I also told him how much I learned working my job at Marie's. Working alone in there was a lot of responsibility. Without missing a beat, he looked at me and said:

"And if you hadn't been working at Marie's, you wouldn't have met *me*!"

Probably not, my love. I'm forever thankful we crossed paths.

We made a habit of cuddling together in his hospital bed and watching more of *Shameless* on Netflix over my cell phone. *Shameless* became a thing with us. We watched it often while he was in the hospital, and as of the point of me writing this, I still have not been able to bring myself to keep watching it.

Once Mark was well enough to go out for a smoke, we discovered his sneakers were lost. So, the hospital gave him some rubber boots to wear, and we took a picture. Rubber boots, a hospital gown, and a smoke. It is a classic to us to this day because it just looked so comical. Yvonne and I always joke that it looks like he's ready to go to war. I originally joked he was going into battle and on to Valhalla. Mark and I both enjoyed Norse mythology, Vikings and such, so it worked out.

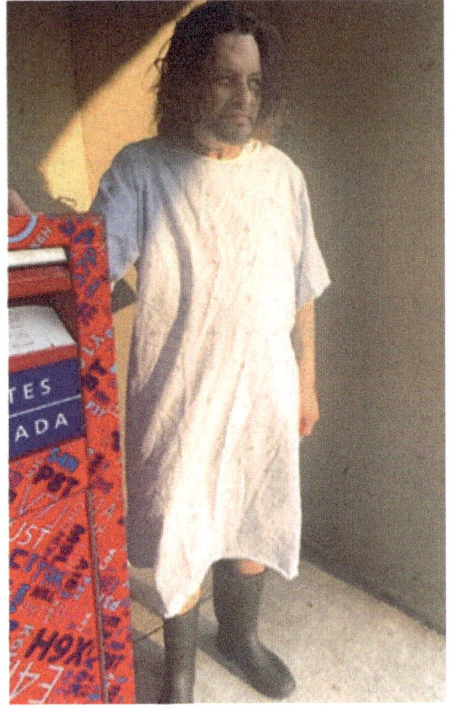

It wasn't long before he got out of the hospital. So, for the third time now, Jesse and I went to look for him because we had no idea where he was. It was evening, and we meandered all over downtown St. John's looking for him. We talked a lot about Mark and how I felt about him. Referring to the concept of soulmates again, Jesse told me that Mark was my lobster. As a massive fan of the sitcom *Friends* as a teen, I thought he was referring to how that was used on the show. He said that while that fit too, he was referring to a Colin Farrell movie called *The Lobster*. I still haven't seen it.

We eventually gave up and I went home. Around 2 am, Mark called me from a phone at his halfway house on Garrison Place, where he lived. When I picked up the phone, he was panicking, wanting to make sure I knew he hadn't "shunned" me after he left the hospital (his words). He told me about how he had been allowed back in his apartment and had fallen asleep. They had to give him a new bed and everything due to the damage from the blood that had been left there. It wasn't far between my apartment and work, so I could easily drop in while going back and forth, which was convenient. I told him I understood, and we agreed we'd see each other later that day.

He came downtown as I was about to finish up my shift at Marie's. I could see him talking with Jesse, Suzie, and a few others across the street. He still had on his hospital bracelet. It was a warm day, and he had on his shorts and a trademark baseball cap as usual. He came to see me in the store, and I told him I'd be out in a few minutes.

When we met up, he had to run down to see an older lady who owned a nearby restaurant. He was paying her back for a loan. She looked at me as he paid her back and asked him, "Girlfriend?"

"Good friend," he replied.

I was taken aback and so questioned him on it.

"You could do so much better than me," he replied.

I told him I didn't want to hear him talk like that. I told him what Barry had told me, and he tried to say he'd never said he loved me...but he had. He invited me back to his apartment, and feeling *very* odd and confused, I went.

What was going on? He seemed so down and was acting weird. While I was there, he ended up in the bathroom for a long time with the door open. I asked him if he was ok, and he said no and closed the door slightly.

Eventually, he came out and sat down on the chair next to his table. I watched him as he tried to inject himself with cocaine. He had horrible veins from years of shooting up and I was shocked as I watched him. He had a hard time and told me afterward that he'd only had a little bit of it because of his bad veins. He certainly didn't act like someone on cocaine, and I believed him.

He laid down on the bed next to me. I told him I was going to look up something on YouTube that I wanted to play for him, but he pointed out that he'd never given me the Wi-Fi code. I had data, so it didn't matter, but he seemed so down. I shot a video clip of him on my phone while he was lying on his bed beside me talking about it. At the end of the video, he stares ahead blankly at the ceiling, almost looking like he was about to cry. Something was very wrong that day, but he did have problems with depression. He said he didn't know what got into him as he hadn't done cocaine in a while, but admitted he wasn't doing well that day at all. He didn't know what got into him that he'd decided to buy some. He never did do it again. I think he was expecting me to run for the hills when I saw him using that needle, but I just sat on the bed and held space for him. He was hurting. I knew enough that it didn't faze me.

He confided some stuff about his upbringing to me that evening. There was a story where his mother, while he was practicing on his guitar as a teen, told him that he couldn't play and might as well stop. It was pretty clear by how he spoke about it, that this stuff really bothered him. I told him the hell with that and to use that as fuel to drive him to play more. Ironically, he wasn't bad at guitar at all and multiple people have attested to that. I told him how Damien had said pretty much the same thing to me, though he initially encouraged it. That spring, I had begun practicing Bob Dylan's *Knocking on Heaven's Door*. I'd use a cover of it for a YouTube dedication to Mark after he passed. I did not practice as much as I should have for a while, as I was too down on myself. I understood how being talked to like this would affect Mark because I'd been through it, though not with a parent.

Damien's opinion had been if I really wanted it, I'd keep going. True... and not true. Sometimes you can get so beaten down in your mind that you just don't have the self-esteem to believe you can do something anymore. People need encouragement, especially children and teens.

Mark picked up his guitar, but his left hand was still messed up, so he handed it over to me. He knew I'd played some over the last couple of years and had my own at home. I love Fleetwood Mac and had previously learned their song, *Don't Stop*. I had been trying to remember how to play it. I struggled for a while, and when I finally got it, he reassured me I could do it and to stop second-guessing myself.

At one point, he showed me a large, mounted print he had leaning up against his wall. He said someone had given it to him, but he never did get it put up. He asked if I'd like to have it, and I told him yes, but that I'd have to bring it home another time. It was a painting called *The Red Maple* by A.Y. Jackson, a famous Canadian painter. It is currently hanging on my living room wall.

Things turned intimate after a while, and he commented that he thought I had the ideal shape for someone who would want to get pregnant. I asked him what he meant, and he said "child-bearing hips." I told him that's an old wives' tale, but I took it as a compliment. He seemed to like my curves and kept running his hand back and forth over where my hip dipped toward my ribs. After having my body put down so much for years, it was almost jarring for me.

A little later, we cuddled in, and I ended up half asleep on his shoulder.

"I love you," he whispered, thinking I was asleep.

The wheels in my head were turning. I didn't know if I should speak up and say, "I love you, too," since, you know, he'd said it because he felt comfortable thinking I was asleep. He obviously was fearful of getting hurt or something. So, I continued to pretend I was napping (which I half was anyhow).

So, Mark, *I love you too*! You knew that anyhow, but I'm saying it here.

Later, when I "woke up," I had to go home to make sure my kitten was okay, as she wasn't used to being alone for so long before. I invited Mark to come with me, but he wasn't up to leaving in the mood he was in. He'd had a rough day emotionally, though he did invite me to stay. Technically he'd been told he was no longer allowed to have guests.

So, we shared one hell of a kiss, and I was gone for the night.

I did come back to see him before I went to work the next day and he seemed in much better spirits. He told me he'd talked to the older woman who lived above him about his girlfriend. It looked like he'd just had a bad day the day before, after all! Sadly, that neighbour has since passed away.

That day was going to be my last day working for Marie's, and I asked him if he would pop down. I wanted to get a picture of us together in the store, just a quick selfie since we'd met there. When I got down to the store, I talked to Barry about how Mark had denied he'd said the stuff he'd claimed from months ago. He looked perplexed and outright shocked. I also told him how he'd said, "You can do so much better than me."

"Actually, he said that to me back then too. I forgot about that till just now, but he did."

When I told him I heard him whisper, "I love you," and how he'd told his neighbour that I was his girlfriend, Barry seemed relieved that he'd admitted it.

"Yeah, he loves you."

It was my usual Saturday night shift, and Mark never showed up. He called me from a phone at Garrison and apologized over and over, telling me how he'd fallen asleep again, and didn't stand me up. I reassured him I understood, as I knew how groggy he could get by now. He asked if I'd come over for the night, so I agreed.

Mom was picking me up that night to drive me home and she wasn't pleased when I told her I was going over for the night. She was leery of the whole thing, and I can't really blame her after Damien, but we got into it in the car. We'd argued once before because she disapproved. I could deal with her not understanding or not approving, but I was upset at how she went about expressing it. I got out of the car when we reached my apartment and went inside for a bit. I spent a little time with my cat...played with her, ensured she had food and water, and then grabbed a cab over to Mark's. I could have walked if it had been during the day, as it was less than a ten minute walk away, but I was not doing that in the dark alone on a Saturday night downtown.

When I got there, what should be on TV but *Wayne's World*. Not just that, but the scene where Cassandra is on the phone and Wayne's wearing her bra, etc. You know, the scene that flashes the words "gratuitous sex scene" on the screen! Oh my, it's such a funny movie! I always got a kick out of it, and it introduced me to the band Queen as a child because of the re-release of the song *Bohemian Rhapsody*. I knew *We Will Rock You* because of hockey games, but I became more familiar with them through *Wayne's World*. Freddie Mercury had just died a short time before the movie's release and I'm a big Queen fan to this day.

We had a good evening, but he was restless and was up most of the night. I'm sure accidentally napping earlier in the evening didn't help. He put on K-Rock. He always had on K-Rock! It's a local classic rock radio station and my favourite to listen to as well. He sat on the chair beside the table with a White Russian in hand. *Angel*, by Aerosmith, came on, and I flashed back to him calling me his guardian angel at St. Clare's when I first told him how I felt. It seemed ironic.

He eventually got some sleep, but he woke up and was very sick for a while the next day. This had also happened at my apartment when he and Jesse first stayed there, but it never seemed to be connected to how much alcohol he'd had. He was having so little of it, just trying to keep withdrawals away. Eventually, he felt like he could eat, so I ordered us some Tim Hortons through Skip the Dishes, which he enjoyed. The small blessings can mean a lot when you are as sick as he was.

8 EVERYTHING I DO

My new job was starting full time at 3 pm the following Monday. Mark called me up, so I went to see him before heading there. No joke, his apartment at the halfway house was covered in vomit by the time I got there. It was on the floor near the bed, making a line toward the door, and even in his bathtub. What he had thrown up, I can only guess, was White Russians. It smelled something like stale chocolate. It's hard to explain, but nothing very stomach-turning. I immediately grabbed the mop, filled a bucket with soapy water, and began cleaning. He told me I didn't need to do that. I had a couple of hours before work and told him there was no way I was leaving him there sick without helping him get it clean. It didn't take long, and then I rested and hung out for a while.

He revealed that he already knew what he wanted to get me for Christmas. That was twice within a few weeks that he'd brought up Christmas and us together. It certainly gave me peace of mind. I had virtually no paranoia that he was in this short term. He was going for the long haul.

"I think you'll like it," he said. I will never know what it was.

He showed me that his feet were swelling badly again. They'd been a bit better since he'd last been in the hospital, but it had returned. He wanted to go downtown with me; so I worked to try and get his boots on him, though it wasn't easy. His feet were swollen with so much water that I felt like the servant who was with the Grand Duke at the end of *Cinderella*, trying to force the glass slipper onto the feet of her stepsisters. He honestly thought he was going to go downtown that day, but he couldn't bring himself to do it afterward.

When I saw him after my shift (before I headed home), he said it was a good thing I'd helped him clean before I left, as one of the employees had been in to check on him. He felt he would have been in trouble. I tend not to think so, as he was sick and he couldn't help that, but he fist-bumped me anyway.

He also told me he'd gone up to the liquor store nearby. He was weak and unsteady, so should never have tried going up there alone, but this is how it is with addictions. It's not even the psychological side, but just the fact alone that he needed his alcohol to not get so sick from withdrawal. He felt it was something he had to do, and he ended up getting hurt.

Well, he had a fall when he went up there. His face was bruised and cut, and he had an even harder time walking. I joked that he looked like Rocky Balboa. We sat down at his table, and he began to confide in me that most of his girlfriends in the past had cheated on him "within, like, three days," as he put it. We talked a lot about him wanting to return to rehab at the Grace Centre in Harbour Grace. He said the program was about a month long.

"Then I got to thinking about you and..." he continued quietly. It seemed painful for him to be vulnerable like he was.

He was scared of leaving me here for fear I'd end up with someone else. I reassured him he didn't have anything to worry about with that whatsoever. I told him I was crazy about him. I still am to this day.

He seemed relieved and leaned in for a kiss. When we touched, he unexpectedly blew a little raspberry on my lips, causing me to laugh. He was so loving and adorable with me. It was always so cute. He went on to say how amazing he felt when he'd gotten out of rehab in December after his last visit there. I told him he needed to go for it and that I'd be waiting for him. I'd even see if I could get out there to visit him while he was there if at all possible, as it was only about an hour away.

He didn't want me to leave and asked me to stay the night, but I had stuff I needed to get done at the house that I'd been neglecting for a while. But then, I wanted to spend time with him so badly. We hated being apart, so I asked him if he'd come over to my place, and he said yes.

Thank God he did.

I called a cab because he was still struggling with walking. When we got to the house, he wanted to watch a movie. He asked if we could watch *Leaving Las Vegas*. It was one of his favourite movies, and he felt it was a realistic depiction of what it's like for alcoholics. Before I tried to find that on digital,

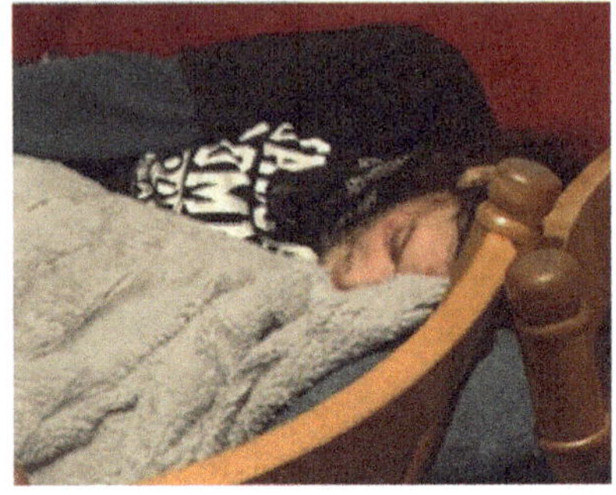

he asked if I could make him some eggs and bacon he'd brought to the house. By the time I made it, he was starting to get sleepy. He ate some but fell unconscious, leaving the rest of the food on his plate on the chair in case he woke up again. The poor man was bushed, so I didn't wake him. I snapped a picture of him cuddling into one of my throws and then went about getting my chores done. Finally, I went to bed and figured he'd come in when he woke up later. I made sure to leave the door open.

I woke up early the next morning and he still wasn't in bed. I kept hearing him coughing from the couch, so I called out to him. He wasn't responding to me and was just coughing from time to time. Something felt very off, so I got up.

I walked into the living room as I was speaking to him, and as I reached the couch, I saw that he was still lying there. His eyes were wide open, but he was not responding to me.

I thought maybe he had something in his throat because of the coughing, but it didn't seem that way as he wasn't acting as if he could even tell I was there talking to him. He just stared blankly ahead at the ceiling.

I pulled him up enough that I was able to sit behind him and sit him upright, which is not easy to do with the dead weight of a grown man. He wasn't holding himself up at all. I grabbed the garbage can I'd left next to him the night before in case he got sick and I started smacking his back. I didn't know what was going on. Choking? It didn't sound like it. He was breathing and just coughing in a weird, unconscious way. Did he need to vomit and couldn't? Why the blank stare? I realized I had to call 911.

When the paramedics arrived, they turned him on his side on the floor. I was sitting on the couch. As they turned him, he vomited up bile. They got me to grab a towel to cover that area of the floor. They weren't sure what was wrong, but they tried to get him to respond, and he was not reacting to anything around him whatsoever, even though his eyes were open. They felt he'd had a seizure, which had also happened when he'd thrown up blood again in June.

After removing the screen, they got him on a stretcher and had to take him out through my living room window. The stretcher wouldn't fit through the kitchen entrance to get out through the porch. I again wasn't allowed to go in the ambulance with him. They told me they were taking him to the Health Sciences Centre this time. I watched them take him and was left alone in a meltdown, not knowing what to do with myself.

I threw the bile-covered towel in the washer and got ready to call work to tell them I wouldn't be in and why. Then called a cab to take me to the hospital. There were numerous people downtown who would say Mark had a stroke. He had never had a stroke—only seizures from alcoholism.

Once I got there, it took a while before I was even allowed in a private waiting room. One of the paramedics from my house was in the registration area and told me many people were working around him at that moment, so I'd have to wait fifteen minutes to a half-hour. It was hours before I even knew what was happening.

I just kept thinking, over and over, how thankful I was that he had been at my house. I got on the phone with friends, trying to pass the time and telling them about everything that had happened. I was scared out of my wits and crying half the time. Someone finally came to me and asked why I was waiting there. When I told them, they took me to a separate room specifically for loved ones. They said the doctor would come to see me there when they were ready to talk to me. It seems I was put in the wrong spot before. Wonderful.

A nurse asked me if I wanted a lunch bag with food in it, and I felt like I could eat something by this point. I had just started eating a chicken sandwich when the doctor came in to talk to me and informed me that Mark had, in fact, had a seizure. They had no idea at this point if he would even be "normal" again.

I was finally brought to a room unlike any hospital room I remember being in. I walked in, and there was blood spatter all over the floor. They'd apparently had a hard time finding veins for his IVs. As I said before, his veins were terrible. He was sleeping and covered in all kinds of medical stuff; I couldn't even tell you what it all was or what it was for. There were giant round lights above his bed like you see on TV in operating rooms. It was unreal to see him like this. I spoke to him, not knowing if he could even hear or understand anything. He was eventually getting moved to the ICU, and they told me there was no point in sticking around as that would take a while. So I reluctantly left and headed downtown to Marie's to let Jesse, Barry, and Suzie all know that he'd had a seizure...again.

For the first few days, I was only allowed to be with him for limited hours due to him being in the ICU and COVID still going on. I went back to work and headed to the hospital as soon as I could afterward every day. I always called as soon as I woke up to ask for updates on his condition. He opened his eyes during the first couple of days, but he wasn't making any sense and his hand motions if he tried eating or drinking were very slow, etc.

At one point, I was saying about having to call a cab to go home.

"Call your dad," he said unexpectedly.

I was surprised in his current state that he could remember my dad had anything to do with taxis as he was pretty spaced.

"My dad passed away in June, remember?"

His face became sad.

"Oh, I'm sorry," he replied glumly as if he were offering me his condolences. He knew in his normal state of mind that my dad had passed away and I was terrified he was never going to be the same.

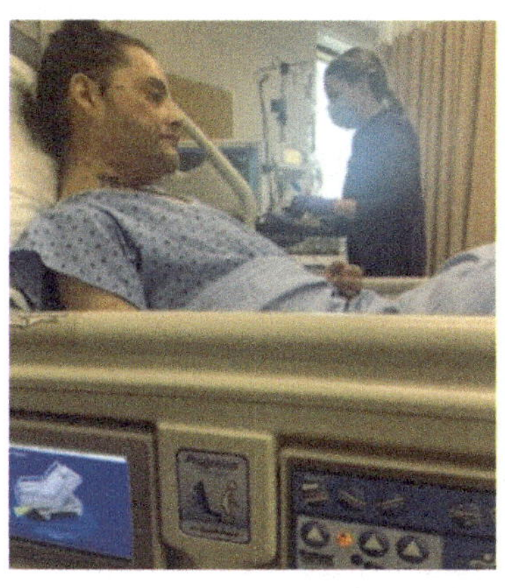

One day, when he was doing a bit better, a social worker came in to chat with me about something.

"I don't want to go to hell," Mark suddenly blurted out while she was there.

I didn't question him about it at that moment, as I knew he was still kind of out of it. I planned to ask him about it later after he eventually got moved up to a room and was out of the ICU. Right now they were trying to get him stabilized better. He told them everything looked wavy and he was starting to hallucinate so they started giving him vodka shots.

Yvonne was on her way here to be with Jesse and hang out with all of us during all this chaos. It wasn't the happiest way for her to arrive and she was getting in on a flight late at night. That afternoon, while on my lunch break, I walked down toward Marie's to emphasize to Jesse not to forget in a drunken stupor to meet her at the airport. I told him I'd kick his ass if he left the poor girl there by herself by accident. Yvonne told me later that I had him trying so hard to remember it. So much so that when he was out of it on the cab ride back after picking her up, he was still reminding himself that I would be pissed if he forgot. She was like, "Dude, I'm right here!" I still get a kick out of that story. I guess I'm scary when I mean business.

During Mark's time in the ICU, my friend Jen and I got to talking and decided to go prayer warrior for him. Neither of us were Christian at the time, but we left messages in spiritual groups that we were in online and called up churches to request prayer for him. It couldn't hurt, right? She called churches in Ohio, and I called a lot in St. John's. I left voicemails for many of them, but some were able to talk to me. Some called me back.

Anyone I spoke to said they absolutely would pray for him. I'd later have voicemails on my phone telling me they got my message and letting me know they'd have the congregation pray for him as well. I have a clip I saved of the Salvation Army Temple here in St. John's saying a prayer for him on their online service that following Sunday.

When Mark was finally moved up to a room, he started to come around more and Jesse brought Yvonne over to see him. She hadn't seen Mark since her first visit here in 2019. Mark and Barry came up with the nickname "Mouse" for her during that visit. She's a tiny little Indigenous woman who likes to change her hair colour practically every few weeks. The nickname is cute, and I think it suits her. Mark could converse with them and such and seemed to be recovering well enough.

One day we were talking about rehab again, and he said he still wanted to go. I decided to ask him why he'd said "I don't want to go to hell" when he was in the ICU. I had brought it up to Jesse already and he had told me he and Mark had conversations in the past about how when Mark died he hoped God would just let him sleep and not send him anywhere. I told him what Jesse had said and asked him why it was that he just wanted to fall asleep.

"I've done a lot of bad shit," he responded.

He feared going to hell and didn't think he was good enough to go to heaven. Growing up in the Christian faith, we both were taught none of us are good enough and fall short. Sin literally means to "miss the mark" and that's the point of repentance and trusting in the Saviour for bearing our sins on the cross. All we can do is try and do our best after that.

"I know you did," I responded, "but you're also sorry. I saw that out of you a long time ago."

I was referring to a conversation we'd had in the store the previous winter. He'd broken someone's window while pissed off with someone else. He was upset with himself because it dawned on him that the person who owned that window wasn't even the person he was angry with.

"You have a good heart, and God is a God of forgiveness, and He knows your heart."

That was one thing I was certain of from church growing up, that if anyone were out there watching us with that much knowledge and power, they'd know our hearts. They'd know how sorry he was. I wasn't sure at this point what I thought of it all. As I've said, I wasn't a Christian at this point in my life, but I knew enough from my past that I hoped it would bring him comfort. But he certainly did get me thinking about it myself.

Mark had plenty of regrets. Later that summer, I asked him what he wanted for his birthday this year.

"A life do-over," he responded.

Oh, that moment you *wish* you had a TARDIS. As I sat there talking with him, the story of the thief on the cross went through my head repeatedly when I'd look at him.

For those unfamiliar with the Bible, it says Christ was crucified between two criminals. One was a thief who acknowledged he deserved his sentence and asked Christ to remember him when He entered His kingdom. Christ responded, because of the man's repentant heart and his faith, that he would be with Him "in Paradise." That's exactly the feeling Mark was giving me. *I did not, and do not, say that lightly*. Mark was very regretful and sorry...and very scared.

He was supposed to appear in court around this time for the broken window incident. He was certain he was going to end up in jail for not being there. I tried to tell him there was no way they were going to do that since he was in the hospital. He wasn't so sure until one day he finally got word the charges were dropped.

He was so miserable from digestive distress that he'd often stick his fingers down his throat and make himself throw up to try and get relief. I always cringed as he'd do that and I can't even imagine what that's like. As I said at the beginning of this story, I've been very sick in the past and would throw up a lot when I had gone through stuff. But to be so miserable from nausea as to make yourself throw up for relief? It was hard to watch him do that. I had always fought against my own nausea.

A few days went by, and things took a sudden downturn when he began to vomit this dark brown liquid again. It certainly wasn't White Russians after a week in the hospital. At first, the staff thought it was probably because he'd had chocolate pudding that day. Mark told me I could call the Recovery Centre for him to check out his options. People usually went there before going to rehab out in Harbour Grace.

He wasn't making any sense the next day when I came in to see him. He was cursing at the nurses and me. There was no variety to it. It was just "FUCK OFF!" He didn't seem lucid while doing it either. It's like he wasn't there anymore. I wrote Yvonne over Facebook, letting her know and sending her a video. Mark seemed to be in pain and spaced out (besides the swearing). They had X-rayed his stomach and done more blood tests, and I told her the doctor was supposed to come in soon. He seemed out of it, just like when he was still somewhat sedated by the medications right after the seizure.

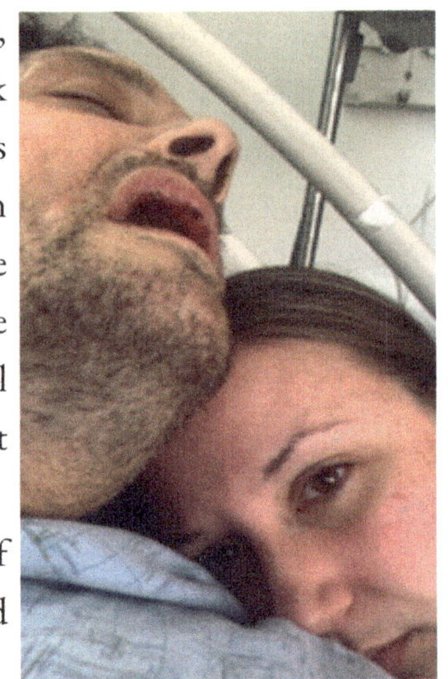

I was lying next to him when one of the residents from the team came in and introduced herself.

"Are you his partner?" she asked.

"Yes."

"He's not doing very well...so we have a room that we could go in. Is that okay with you?"

This was when I got really nervous.

We made some small talk as we made our way through the hallway.

"It's just here on the side," she motioned toward a room with a table and some chairs.

She informed me that the doctor overseeing Mark's care would be in soon. I had my phone recording at this point because I wasn't sure what the doctor would tell me, and I wanted to ensure I didn't forget any possibly important details. So, the following is copied right from that.

"So, Mr. Cambers is *very* sick," the doctor said after sitting down with me finally.

"Oh yeah...I know that."

"And he has multiple medical problems. He has taken a turn for the worse." The words hit me like a ton of bricks. The man had gotten right to the point in a very abrupt way. He felt cold and distant.

"Is there any way he's going to bounce back from it?" I asked nervously, trying to remain hopeful.

"There's a low chance, but I think there's a greater chance that he will get worse. Right now, if his heart were to stop, or he were to stop breathing, he'd need a tube and to be put in the ICU. I'm not sure if that would be useful long term. He has many issues that have only gotten worse over time. I would like to make a suggestion that we do what we can to treat him medically, but not send him to the ICU or put tubes in to help him breathe or any of these artificial things. Because I don't think it would improve his quality of life."

"Is it the cirrhosis got worse or—"

"Everything is getting worse with time," he interrupted me.

"Before this seizure happened, he was talking about going into the rehab in Harbour Grace again, and I'm just wondering, is there any chance that—"

"Well, there's always a small chance," he interrupted me again. "But you know, his mental status is not good. It's unfortunate. The body can only take certain things, and after a while of constant or repetitive insults to the body, the body begins to fail." I started to burst into tears, but he paid no mind as he continued. "So, he comes in the first time, he bounces back. But every time, the body can't bounce back as much as it used to."

"I had a conversation with him, and he was so serious about going to rehab, I just kept praying for him to get one more chance."

"Oh yes, well, we hope that he will," he replied. The woman who had brought me into the room picked up a box of tissues and handed it to me to wipe my eyes and nose. I was a mess.

Eventually, I was allowed to go back to the room. Unsure if Mark could understand me, I tried to tell him what was happening, but he just continued to swear and stare off into the ceiling. I told Jesse and Yvonne, and they planned to come up to see what was happening.

"Health Sciences Centre, 4 South A, room 174," I told Yvonne over Facebook. When they arrived, Suzie had come up from downtown with them. She was somewhat loud and pretty upset at what she was seeing. She had rosary beads and put them around his neck. She was irate, though not at any particular person, just at the situation. This was her way of coping, I suppose. It was hard for everyone. They hung around a couple of hours before Jesse and Yvonne headed back to my place. They agreed to look after Lumi while I was at the hospital.

By half past nine that night, I'd had a short nap next to him, but my head was *absolutely killing me* from all the crying I had done. They were giving him a substance called lactulose by enema to try and get the ammonia and toxins off his brain.

When the liver can't clear your blood, you can get a condition that's called hepatic encephalopathy. The lactulose makes you have bowel movements, so you can clear the excess toxins and hopefully be able to think straight again. At this point in the evening, he wasn't swearing anymore; he was just making noises. Things got really messy and real terrifying after this. You've been warned.

He had a bowel movement in the diaper that they had on him. At 2 am, he was getting another enema; and as he was turned on his side, he began to have a movement. While this was happening, he began projectile vomiting that brown liquid again at the same time. They moved him onto his back when he stopped so they could try and get him cleaned up, thinking it was a one-time thing. Then it started happening again while he was on his back, so they had to turn him back on his side quickly. There was so much vomit that it went all over the floor. That's when I started to freak out. It was becoming too much for me. I felt like I was about to lose my mind, freaking out inside and feeling like I could faint. It wasn't so much feeling sick from seeing him vomit. As I've said...once in the not-so-distant past, I would have been very nauseated by this. But this time it was different. I left the room, went out into the hallway, and ended up sitting on the floor in front of the nursing station. The nurses asked me if I needed a glass of water or a blanket and brought me both. I just sat there trying to get a grip on myself while everyone was in his room cleaning everything up and trying to stabilize him. I feel like my blood pressure must have dropped at least a bit from what I'd just seen happen. It felt like it, anyhow. I must have been white as a ghost.

When they eventually let me back in the room, they had put him on antibiotics just in case the liquid was from his bowels...but they really weren't sure what it was. They also gave him some medication in case he had a GI bleed. They told me if he was stable enough, they'd do an endoscopy in the morning. There were all kinds of IV bags hanging from the pole. There wasn't room for any more, it was full. I didn't lie on the bed next to him with so many IV tubes and the chance he might throw up again. I sat in his wheelchair and fell asleep in it, covered in the blanket the nurses had given me. I woke up later in the morning when he started throwing up again, though this time only once. My neck was killing me from falling asleep in the chair, so I told the nurses I needed somewhere to rest. They showed me a room with a couch; it was dark and looked like it wasn't used for much of anything anymore. I called Mark's dad and spoke to him briefly, and then lay down to get some rest. I had maybe two hours of sleep.

When I woke up, I wrote Yvonne on Facebook, letting her know that Mark was back to saying "ouch" and "fuck," so it seemed he was becoming more responsive again. It appeared that the lactulose they had given him might have been reversing the toxin build-up. I started to feel somewhat positive he'd be coming out of this and decided to take the risk of going home for a few hours. I briefly spoke to Yvonne and Jesse before zonking out in my bed for three hours. Then I was up and back to the hospital again. He was talking more, but not making complete sense yet.

The next day he was better still. We were able to make conversation, but some stuff that came out of his mouth still wasn't making any sense. He'd ask me to hold him at random while still sounding like he was in some pain. Over the next few days, he started to get to the point where he was fairly normal until he became groggy and needed sleep. Then some nonsense would begin to come out again, but not anything significant.

I often grabbed him treats from the snack bar that he wanted. He gave me the PIN to his debit card and often told me to pick out whatever I wanted as well. He usually wanted a chocolate glazed donut from the Tim Hortons downstairs and yogurt. He loved his Iced Capps too. It was a bit of change from all the Ensures he was drinking, though he did love those.

"I feel better now," he said one night after I returned with the snacks from downstairs.

"Why? Because you have non-hospital food?" I asked.

"No, because you're here. If it weren't for you, I'd be fucked," he replied.

He reached out for a hug at one point, so I bent over the bed and held him. I could feel the scruff of his cheek against mine.

"It's fucked up in here, man," he said sadly, playing with my hair as we hugged. He ended up touching my left breast with his other hand.

"Copping a feel?" I joked.

"Yeah," he replied, then "honked" it twice!

Yeah, he was more himself than he had been in a while. Surprisingly, he'd gotten sick once that time, but it wasn't the dark stuff.

Unfortunately, he was not well enough to leave yet. A social worker with the hospital talked to me in private. She wanted me to convince Mark to sign papers for a young adult nursing home. She said that he was incontinent with peeing and pooing and how he couldn't yet feed himself again. He had *terrible* tremors and would drop the utensils or miss his mouth while trying to eat, barely even able to sit up in the chair...though she wasn't saying he'd never regain those abilities. I initially tried to convince him, but he said it's his life and he will do what he wants. I explained to him it was only a precaution in case he needed the nursing home care. If he recovered, I had been told he could still leave and live normal as he did before. Well, as normal as it would get with liver cirrhosis.

I told him I didn't want him to leave the hospital too soon and get worse again...or the very real possibility he would die if he didn't handle this right. I told him that Jesse and I had joked once that Mark and I were like the movie *Titanic* but on land.

"You're the classy lady, and he's the dirty street kid," Jesse laughed.

We were just joking around at the time, but I started crying while telling Mark about it. I told him I was scared I'd end up like Rose at the end of that movie...doing all the things they'd talked about doing, but doing them without Jack. He said he'd sign the papers. The social worker said it was his best chance at getting well, should anything else happen.

I stayed overnight that night at his request. The nurses let me stay on the bed with him. Jesse and Yvonne continued to stay at my place and watch Lumi. It was Regatta Day here the next day, so there was a chance I'd not have to go to work if it went ahead, as it was a holiday.

And if I did have to go to work, I didn't have to be there till the afternoon. So, I cuddled in behind him on the bed. I ended up having to go to work, but I told him I'd see him soon.

Things seemed to be going well until I came in the next day. He was in a pair of scrubs and lying outside the covers on his bed.

Looking somewhat healthy compared to before, he told me they said he was supposed to be getting out and was mad because they hadn't let him leave yet. I had my doubts about this, and as it turned out, he was trying

to leave, but they didn't want him to. For well over an hour and a half, I tried to convince him to stay. He got up off the bed and started trying to unfold the walker that was in the room. At one point, he bent down, saying he was trying to get his sock under the hospital bed, but there was absolutely nothing there. He fell over and continued to sit on the floor. I pleaded with him that if he wasn't going to trust the hospital staff that he should stay in there, to please trust me.

"Do you trust me?" I asked, seriously wondering at this point.

"Of course I trust you," he replied, barely over a whisper.

I tried to reason with him. If he trusted me, why didn't he trust me saying he should stay in the hospital? He was a strong man and had such a strong spirit to make it through everything he had in his life and live the way he lived. I think he felt invincible to some extent, and the rest of us even began to feel that way. He always came out okay.

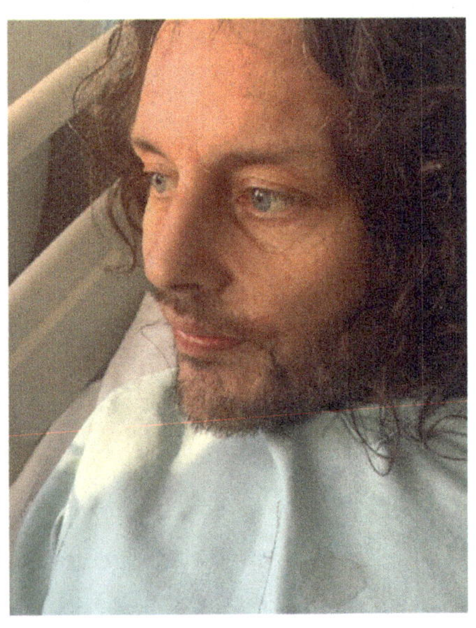

This last incident was alarming. I'm sure it sounds terrible reading it, but seeing it was so much worse. To this day, I still deal with not only PTSD about the loss of him but everything that I saw him go through up till the time he left this world.

He eventually calmed down and agreed to get back in bed. I snapped a picture of him as the sunlight hit one side of his face. Sadly the sunlight didn't show up well, but it's still one of my absolute favourite pictures of him. It's the best picture of those *gorgeous* blue eyes; he looks so angelic. People who knew him casually may laugh at that, but those that really knew his heart realized he just had a broken wing (so to speak). I mean that and I know others who would attest to the same thing.

Over the coming days, he was more and more himself. They gave him some benzodiazepines and vodka shots while in the hospital to keep him from withdrawing. One day he wanted to call his brother, so they had a nice chat over speaker phone. He asked if it was okay if he prayed for Mark out loud right there, and Mark was all for it.

Another day I had him talk to my friend Jen over the speaker phone as well. She told him about all her kids (all eleven of them. Yes, you read right) and how they could be little terrors...in a funny way, most of the time. He had the *biggest* open-mouthed smile on his face while listening to the stories. You could tell he was reminiscing on his childhood and getting into trouble. He got such a kick out of the tales she told.

I took him out front one night for a smoke in his wheelchair, and we stopped at a bench so I could sit down too. We talked about what the doctor had told me when he wasn't doing well. I played him the recording I'd taken.

"He's talking about me?" he asked, after hearing the doctor talk about how he didn't feel he would come out of it this time.

"Yeah."

He didn't want to keep listening to it too long. He was freaked out and pissed off at the doctor for "scaring his girlfriend." But I told him it really was bad. I understood why the doctor told me what he did, but at the same time, they hadn't even tried the lactulose yet. I questioned why the doctor couldn't try that and then talk to me if it didn't work, but what's done is done now. When Mark's father called me he told me that he felt it was a roller-coaster. They'd also told him he wasn't going to pull through.

Another man in a wheelchair, who had been there some distance away with a couple of others, came up to us. He looked to be around our age group and was covered in tattoos himself. Of all things he started talking about... he started talking about praying. At first glance, you would not think he was someone religious, not the stereotype anyhow. He started talking about talking to God and how you really have to mean it, how you can't just talk to Him when you need something, etc. He began to tell us how he was a quadriplegic, and now he's not, though he was still in a wheelchair and told Mark that he was lucky to have me.

"I know I am," Mark replied.

Then the man commented to him that I'm a beautiful woman before turning to me and saying I was lucky to have Mark too, and how he seems like a nice guy.

"You *can* get better again, but you have to put the work in," he said, turning to Mark again.

Mark didn't seem to like talking to this guy very much. I think he just wanted to be left alone to relax and have his smoke. But you could tell that he had him thinking.

9 NOT WITHOUT YOU

Mark finally got out of the Health Sciences Centre on the eleventh of August. He called me from Garrison Place and asked me to come over. When I got there, he was sitting at the kitchen table in his overalls and a baseball cap. He said Penny (not her real name), one of the workers for the building, wanted to talk to us about something. I was a little confused. He still didn't have his bag back from The Gathering Place from all those weeks earlier and though I'd tried multiple times, it never worked out. He still didn't have his cell phone, so he had me call her and let her know I was there.

When she got there, she asked if we could come downstairs to a meeting room in the basement. Mark had a White Russian. He said he was still serious about quitting but the drinks were still in his fridge when he got back, and the temptation had been too much for him. He was pacing himself, however, and was pretty much completely sober.

She began to talk to us about how everyone at Garrison was concerned about him staying there because he'd be alone. They didn't want him to have a seizure, and no one know he was in there in need of help. They also worried about the legal repercussions should that happen. She said he wasn't being evicted, but to give it a couple of weeks to see how he did and asked if it would possibly be okay if he went to stay with me. We both were more than okay with that, and I let her know that when I couldn't be there with Mark that Jesse, or Yvonne, or maybe both of them would be.

Yvonne and I had bounced around the idea of the four of us getting a place together, so I told Mark about that since we were discussing his living situation. My lease was going to be up in September, so if we were all going to do it, now was the time to start looking.

"I'd be down for it," he responded.

We talked for a while about everything, mostly about sobriety and going to rehab. He still wanted to do it, but he voiced to us that he was concerned that should he get completely sober, he'd lose his current friends and have to start from scratch again. He'd asked Jesse to get sober with him in the past. Funny enough, they'd both asked each other on different occasions; it just hadn't happened yet.

"Well, I don't drink," I piped up, trying to be positive for him.

"Yeah, that's a big plus!" he responded, looking at me with the cutest playful grin.

When we returned to his apartment, Penny gave us time to get some of Mark's things that he wanted to bring. Everything was pretty much ready when she came back, but he went into the fridge and took out a large bottle of vodka. I had thought there had only been the one with a little bit left, but I was wrong. I asked him if he would leave it, but he didn't want to. I got up, stood next to him, and tried to convince him not to take it with him.

"You told me about all these times that people downtown pissed you off...how much you wanted to punch some people. But that right there," I said, motioning to the bottle, "that's stolen more from you in your life than any human being. Will you *please* pour it down the sink?"

You could hear his breathing intensify as I tried to convince him he should pour it out. He kept staring at the bottle, gripping it intensely in his hand. This moment felt like it went on much longer than it probably actually did, but it was still powerful. I'd been around alcoholics, but this was something else. He ended up keeping it, but didn't bring it with him. If he needed it, he'd just get it later and only brought the one that had a small bit left.

"You almost had me pouring it down the sink," he told me later that night, sounding a little taken aback himself.

"It was *very* apparent how much love he had for you," Penny would later tell me after he passed. "I could see the struggle in his face for the first time. No one was ever able to do that to him. You couldn't see me because you were facing him, but I had tears in my eyes watching you guys because I'd never seen that struggle before you, *not like that*."

Before we left, she got his key card off him to make sure he didn't return without telling anyone. We headed outside, and she said she was going to let some of the others who worked there know that Mark was leaving. Friends who lived in neighbouring apartments began coming out to see what was happening.

He sat on a set of steps that oddly led to nowhere and lit up a smoke. There were people up on the balcony who'd come out to see him, as well as down below where we were. It felt like a scene out of a movie. It was an overcast day, and I can still see him sitting there talking to everyone about everything he'd been through over those last few weeks.

"I don't know how I landed a girl like her. I'm a drunk with no teeth," he joked in a self-deprecating manner as he looked over at me. He had no problem broadcasting that I was his lady, and he did it proudly. I wasn't used to that.

Later Jesse told me that Mark would say similar things to him every time I left for work while they were still at the apartment. If there was something I can say for sure, it was that *Mark appreciated me*. He let not only me know, but everyone else he spoke to. There were no silly games with him like I'd dealt with sometimes with exes in the past. Some would not always be open with friends about the relationship for a long time, leaving me to wonder if they were hiding it for a reason (and some were). I tried to make sure he knew he meant just as much to me. I loved him, and it was hard if his illness got intense, but who wouldn't find it challenging? We just always wanted to be together, so sticking with him through everything that was happening was just natural.

He talked a bit about his situation and how he was coming to stay with me. In hindsight, I don't think any of the people living and working there would realize it would be the last time they'd see him. The whole scene is burned into my brain, and I can easily picture it even now. It was one of those moments you don't realize would be so memorable until much later.

They decided to give us a cab voucher to get to my house. When we got inside, we told Jesse and Yvonne about what was going on. We devised a plan so Mark would ideally never be left completely alone...at least not for very long.

That evening we watched some movies, starting with *Cry Baby*. It's an early nineties movie musical by John Waters I'd seen as a kid, with Johnny Depp as the title character. It's hilarious. Mark couldn't recall seeing it before, but he enjoyed it. I kept catching people off guard by filming and taking pictures. I took a quick selfie of myself with Mark and caught him in the middle of chewing. He's probably looking over my shoulder right now, willing me to remove it from this book. But then again, maybe not. He knew how to laugh at himself.

The next few days were a bit of a blur of movies and music. We watched *Splash*, *Ninja Turtles* (the 1990 version, or what I like to call *the best version*), *Pirates of the Caribbean*, *Ghostbusters*, *Lord of the Rings*, and *My Girl*. He was happy when we decided we wanted to watch that last one.

"*My Girl's* an awesome movie!" he enthusiastically blurted out.

He was definitely in touch with his feelings. It feels ironic in hindsight if you know how that story ends.

We also watched *The Crow*, but there were so many more. The night we watched it, he left to lay down in the bedroom before the very end. I'm giving you a spoiler alert if you still haven't seen the movie after all these years. Eric's dead fiancée, Shelly, comes to take him to the other side. It seemed like it might have been triggering for him with all of the stuff going on with his illness. I still remember hearing the song, *It Can't Rain All the Time* by Jane Siberry during the end credits as I headed into the bedroom to cuddle with him. I still think of him when I hear it to this day.

Yvonne and I sometimes put on movies when the guys were both asleep. We decided to put on *The Chipmunk Adventure* one night. We sat on the floor painting and singing along with all the tunes. Mark was in the bedroom with the door open, and Jesse was passed out on the couch. Jesse commented later he could remember stirring vaguely and thought it was a fever dream. There's twelve years difference between me and Yvonne, but she knew most of the movies I grew up with as well.

Another night we watched the movie *Ghost*, with Demi Moore and Patrick Swayze. I always got a kick out of Whoopi Goldberg in that movie. She totally deserved her Best Supporting Actress Oscar for the role. She was so funny. When the movie was over, we put on something else, and Mark fell asleep next to me on the couch for a while. When he woke up, he seemed panicked.

"Can you see me?" he asked me.

"Yeah..."

We were all very confused.

He seemed relieved and said he'd been having a nightmare after watching the movie. He said that he was invisible and none of us could see him. This still haunts us. It was *very* eerie for us since he was so sick, and even eerier now that he's gone.

It wasn't all morbidly sad though. One night we went into the bedroom to have time alone, and Mark started joking around. He sat on the bed and started talking in this super hillbilly voice about the "damn kids," began complaining about them, and so on. He must have gone on and on for at least a half-hour. He started referring to me as the grandma to his grandpa, so I began to join in as his hillbilly wife. "Grandma and Grandpa" were cranky old buggers. I wish I had hit record on my phone.

The southern accent always came naturally to me for some reason. Jesse and Yvonne started laughing in the living room while listening to us. I was cracking up the whole time. It was one of the funniest moments of my life, I laughed so much. What a ham he was. He was so funny. I will always wish we could have grown old together.

During this period, I couldn't tell you exactly when some stuff happened or in what order. The days are blurred together in some respects, but it was either the day after he got out of the hospital or the next day that we headed to his pharmacy on Queen's Road. We had to pick up prescriptions that had been called in for him from the hospital. They informed us that some were not covered, so we only picked up the ones that were.

We stopped briefly and sat down next to Gower Street United Church. He got tired so quickly being out of the hospital for such a short time, but he was otherwise doing well. It was great that he was able to walk to and from the pharmacy at all. We had once talked about how even though we both loved living in St. John's, we wanted to get out of town, away from everything and everyone. He began to talk about wanting to leave again. He was exhausted and wanted to be somewhere quiet. I asked him if he was planning to try and leave.

"Not without you," he replied.

I told him it was best we stay in town because his health was so bad, and you don't want to get stuck far from a hospital in his state. To this day, I wish I could have taken him to the Bonavista peninsula, where most of my family comes from. On my mother's side, my grandma comes from the *town* of Bonavista, while on my dad's side, my grandpa had family in both King's Cove and Tickle Cove (I know, cute name, right?). We also wanted to visit L' Anse aux Meadows on the Northern Peninsula, where there is an old Viking settlement. There were a lot of things we planned to do...someday.

When we returned, I realized the lactulose was not in with the medications. This was definitely an essential medication that he needed. It was the same substance they'd given him at the Health Sciences Centre to give him bowel movements and keep the toxins off his brain. I called the pharmacy and asked them how much it was since it wasn't covered. It was under twenty dollars, so I told him I'd get it for him. It was too important that he have that one, so I headed back afterward to pick that up.

Every day at home, I helped make sure he remembered to take all his medicine: lactulose, potassium, his heartburn meds, and Seroquel. There are probably more I'm forgetting. Some, like lactulose, he had to take more than once a day. It was crazy to see him take the lactulose orally all the time with no reaction. It's notorious for being disgustingly sweet, and typically people have a hard time choking it down. I always kept track of his medications and ensured he didn't take too much or too little. Most of it was at bedtime.

Bedtime was our alone time and we rarely went to sleep immediately. One night, I was trying to get something out of the bottom drawer of my dresser right next to the bed when Mark decided to offer up his two cents.

"I love your big butt," he commented playfully as he sat on the edge of the mattress.

"Big flabby butt," I joked. I was self-deprecating whether it was true or not. I didn't like myself, and I'm still working on it.

"*I love it*," he said, then bent over on the bed and kissed the little area of skin between my shirt and pants as I continued to search my drawer.

Many men don't realize how much the little things they say and do can help a woman feel better about herself. Though we should learn to feel secure on our own, a little help doesn't hurt. It also helped to know that Mark had a thing for older women...near his age or even older than him. So I wasn't worried if he had lived that he'd ever trade me in for someone in her twenties as I got old! Just kidding!

Over the coming days, Yvonne and I continued to check Facebook Marketplace for rentals to see if we could all get an apartment. We wanted to stay in the downtown area, ideally.

"Find a place with a tub," he piped up. My place only had a shower.

"Why?"

"We can take a bubble bath together!"

I know I've said this many times already but...he was so cute.

We were all very interested in this one place, but it sadly didn't work out. He turned to me on the couch one night and whispered so that Yvonne and Jesse didn't hear.

"Honestly, I'd be happy if it were just the two of us."

So, when there was continued difficulty finding a place, we eventually gave up on looking for a new apartment. We decided that I would talk to the property management company about Mark moving in.

One night, as I was spooning him in bed with my arm around his chest, he grabbed my hand and kissed my fingers.

"You mean the world to me, and you *always will*. No one's ever been there for me like you have."

I've never forgotten that moment. It was sweet, but also sad because it gave me a sense of how alone he must have felt for a long time. He'd been everywhere and knew a lot of people. It kind of shocked me, but I understood. It was just different with us.

One evening around this time, I painted a picture of the moment I just mentioned. It was a painting that he actually got to see before passing, though I'd go on to do much more. All the artwork in this book is mine unless otherwise stated. I didn't put too much detail in it, like his tattoos and such. I also used different colours for the room to make it pop. It was just a simple representation of that night using gouache paint that Yvonne had brought to Newfoundland with her. We were always doing art together.

Mark and I cuddled all the time. In our bed...or a hospital bed...on the couch...it didn't matter. We were glued to each other. Another night he was so sick. I wasn't sure exactly what spurred it on, I guess the cirrhosis, but it was terrible. I was lying in the room with him, and he just kept throwing up. It was exhausting to the point we both sort of just gave up. I had to put towels on the floor, under and around the garbage can. He was so unwell and didn't always...aim perfectly. Jesse came into the room at one point and looked at the floor.

"Wow, that's disgusting," he commented.

I know it's gross, but it's the reality of how sick the liver cirrhosis made him. It was bad, but at least there was no strong smell again. I'm not sure why it hardly ever smelled, but I thank God it didn't because it would have been harder for me to handle.

Things had calmed down for a while, and he turned toward me and cuddled into the nape of my neck. It wasn't long after we wrapped our arms around each other when I started to feel him necking me. You have got to be kidding me...was he starting to get frisky after everything he'd been through?

Yes, yes, he was.

There was no mistaking the fact when he began to suck on my ear lobe. We never kissed on the lips under those circumstances for obvious reasons, though. I'll never forget that even during all that gross sickness, we both still wanted each other regardless of everything that was going on. It was a very powerful moment if you can imagine. As I've said before, I'd always been so phobic. It was a miracle to me that he could still make me feel that way and that he was feeling that way, even while he was feeling so sick.

In the end, we were hoping for a much bigger miracle.

Mark's birthday was coming up soon, and I wanted to pick up some things for him. I got in touch with Yvonne while on my break at work and asked her if she wanted to come to the mall with me. Since Jesse's birthday was at the end of the month, she figured she might get some shopping done too. She stayed with Mark for the afternoon, and they had a heart-to-heart about different things...about me, Jesse, mortality, and health-related stuff. She told me later that he'd said at one point that he didn't know how much time he had with me, but wanted to *make every moment count*. He was also scared for me that everyone might disappear if he ended up passing away. Mostly Jesse, since Mark was worried that he would start travelling again if he passed and that Yvonne would go back to Ontario if he left. Yvonne promised Mark she intended to stay around so I wouldn't be alone should anything happen. He wanted to be sure I'd be okay. She had no intention of returning to Ontario anytime soon anyhow. Like so many who come to Newfoundland, when she came out here, it began to feel like home to her.

When we were at the mall, Mark was left alone at the house as we didn't know where Jesse was. It was only a couple of hours, so we figured it would be okay. When we got back, we encountered a strange sight. A drawer from the freezer was taken out and lying on our bed, with nothing in it. Lumi's cat bed had been moved across the room next to the couch, and Mark's garbage can was tipped over. He'd gotten sick in it, so some of it was on the floor. Things were generally a mess, and he was lying on the couch looking very spaced. I immediately went to him and sat down, asking what had happened.

"I'm ashamed," he said.

He then proceeded to curse and said all kinds of things that didn't make sense. He said nasty things to me that were totally out of his character, and

I began to realize he was having another emergency and was in need of more lactulose than he had been drinking.

He called me a couple of expletives while in this state, and even though I knew he was not in his right mind, it ended up hurting my feelings. I had tears forming in my eyes, so I made my way to the kitchen to try and escape it briefly. I just needed a moment to get myself together when suddenly he blurted out very loudly:

"*I love you Krista*!"

I turned around in disbelief because it was like he wasn't there...then he was...and immediately he was gone again.

When I turned around again to question him about it, he was right back to not being himself. It was the weirdest thing, as he was not himself at all. If I hadn't had Yvonne there to hear it too, I would have thought I imagined him yelling out "I love you" between different rooms like that.

I don't know if maybe he was scared that I was leaving him for cursing at me because I went out to the kitchen or what may have spurred it on.

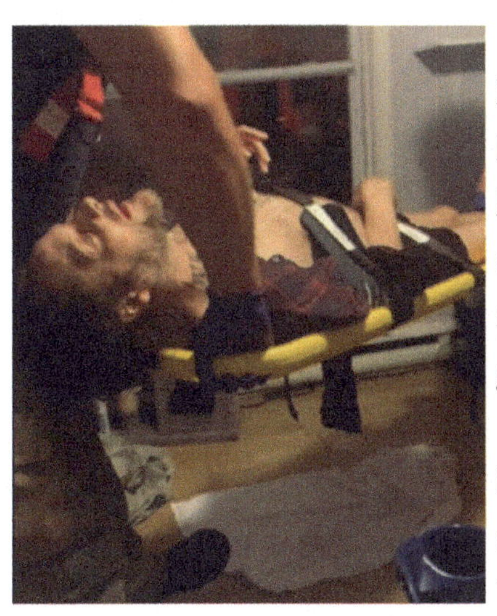

Yvonne reassured me that it had happened and that I wasn't going crazy. It had shocked her too. It was just weird how he blurted it out in the middle of being otherwise completely gone mentally. As quickly as he said it, he was gone again just as fast.

We called the ambulance, but then he also gave them a hard time; cursing at them, yelling, and being very irritable. They again had to take him out through the living room window on a stretcher. I always documented this stuff to show him later, after weird or concerning things had happened a few times.

As usual, I couldn't go with him in the ambulance, and they told me to call the hospital before heading over to make sure they had him in a bed.

When I got to St. Clare's, they brought me into emergency and told me they had to sedate him this time, as he had started swinging at them when they arrived. That's another nasty part of hepatic encephalopathy...it not only makes you confused with impaired judgment, but you can also get very angry as well.

Below: Mark sedated at St. Clare's at about half past two in the morning.

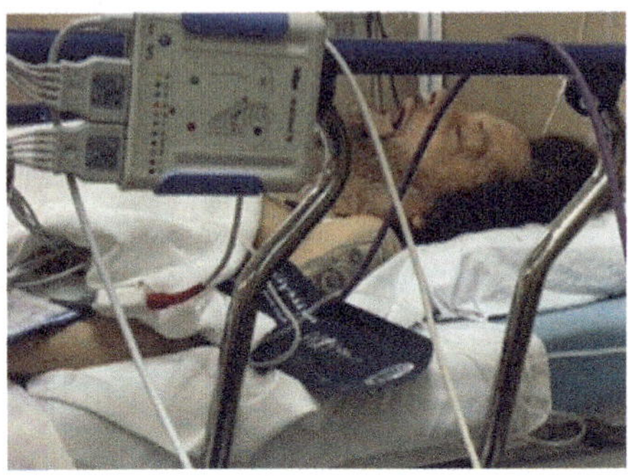

I sat next to him, watching him sleep and worrying yet again if we were fighting a losing battle with his body.

We had been confident that he could get help, get sober, and hopefully get on a waiting list for a new liver. But it felt like trying to beat the clock, and he was running out of time.

10 LIVING ON A PRAYER

Mark had been trying to get into the Recovery Centre, but beds were never available. Now here he was in the hospital again and it was becoming apparent that his health may not allow for this to become a reality.

By the next day, after a lactulose enema again, he'd regained his mind. He couldn't remember much, but he could remember small bits like being mean toward me. It wasn't a complete blackout like at the Health Sciences, so when we got home and found him in that state, he was luckily not too far gone.

When I left, I went home and made him his birthday cake (vanilla, because it was his favourite). For whatever reason, I decided to put on the filmed anniversary concert of *The Phantom of the Opera* on blast as I baked while we hung out. I asked Yvonne to help give some thoughts on what to put on the cake. I had put a middle finger for the obvious reasons you've already read about. She put the anarchy symbol, and I had picked a Viking rune due to our shared interest in the Norse. I added a note in icing saying, "Happy birthday, you tough muthafucka!" Hey, don't say I didn't warn you in the beginning about the language!

We all went to the hospital to see Mark the next day after I got off of work, bringing cake, candy, gifts, and cards. We had to run back to the house briefly first to get it all before heading to the hospital. Bon Jovi's *Living on a Prayer* came on the radio while we were on the way there in the taxi, and so Yvonne, Jesse, and I began to belt it out loudly in the backseat. I think the driver got a kick out of us.

Mark had a hankering for McDonald's while we were at the hospital, so we had some delivered there. He got his usual, the McDouble with no onions, no pickles. Heck no, he hated them. We ordered McDonald's way too much that summer, and these days, it's hard for me to eat it because we had it too much. Mark was always asking if he could have a McDouble.

For gifts, I gave him a new Iron Maiden t-shirt and wireless earbuds so he could listen to music.

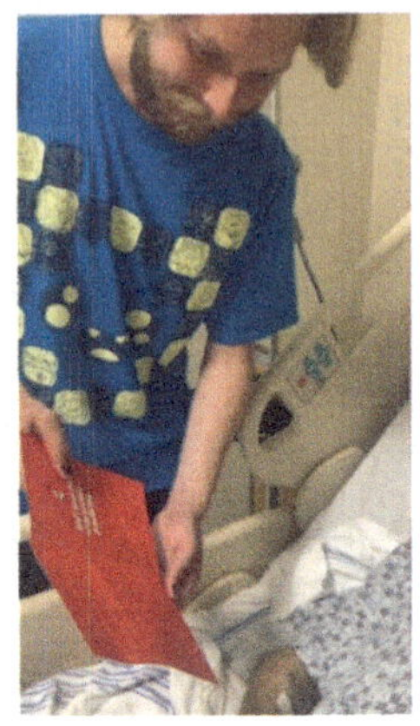

Jesse was there most of the time and read the cards out loud, starting with his, then one from Suzie, and finally mine. He misread a few words, but told us it was due to having some form of dyslexia. It was so comical when he got to reading my card.

When Yvonne and I went to the mall to pick up everything, I'd found a group of cards with humour that totally suited Mark. When I saw this one, we both knew it was the perfect one for Mark and me. It had a nostalgic sixties photo of a woman and her cat on the front. It said: "Happy Birthday from me and my pussy." When we opened it up, it said: "Oh and happy birthday from my cat too!" I ended up putting "Lumi" next to that in brackets. Mark had the biggest smile on his face as Jesse read it out loud to him, "Happy Birthday from Krista and her pussy!" The card was totally worth it. Below the silliness, I inserted my handwritten note to him.

"You are an amazing human being, and you are so strong. You can win this battle. You have many more birthdays yet. I hope I get to share them with you. You are so loving and affectionate toward me... you make me feel safe and cared for. I will always do what I can for you. My dream is you healthy & happy...being able to travel and have fun together. Love always." I added an infinity symbol at the end.

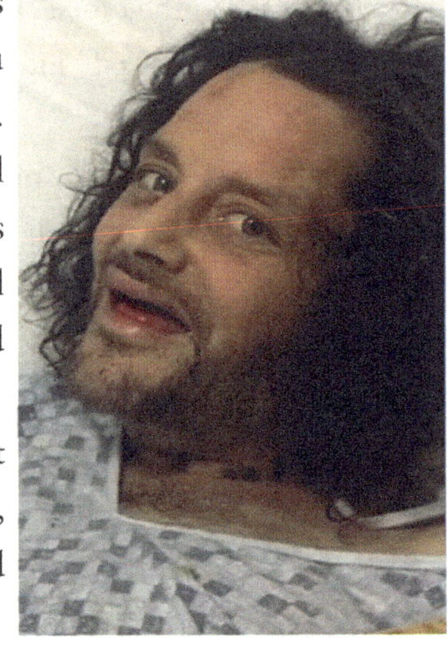

"Thank you," he said as he reached out for a hug. I leaned over the bed, hugged him, and we kissed. He seemed so at peace and happy.

We had some cake, and then Yvonne and I stuck around a little longer after Jesse had left.

Overall, he seemed to have a happy birthday. As happy as it can get from a hospital bed, I suppose.

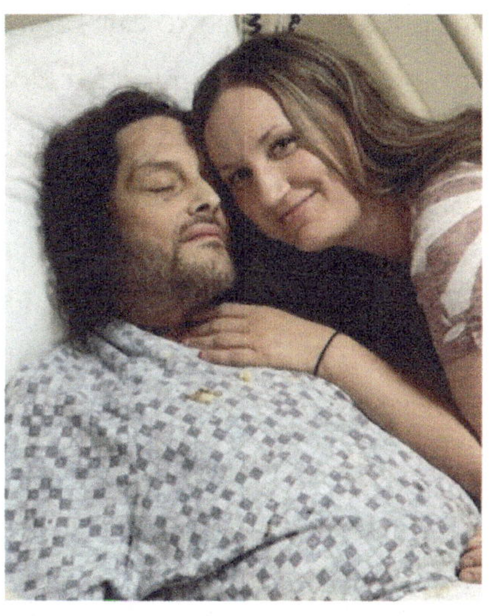

After Jesse left, Yvonne took a few pictures of us. I love this one picture she took. He looks so contented and peaceful with his eyes closed and our heads together. It melts my heart. We kept giving each other kisses, but she wasn't fast enough and we didn't know when she was snapping. Somehow, she did not catch even one out of the three pictures she took. Oh well, we liked what we got either way.

He was also very happy that I was able to bring him his cell phone finally. We had tried to get his things back from The Gathering Place a few times. "Penny" (from Garrison) finally got it all back and dropped it off to me at the apartment. So, he also got his phone back for his birthday too, and everything else that had been left there in his backpack back in June.

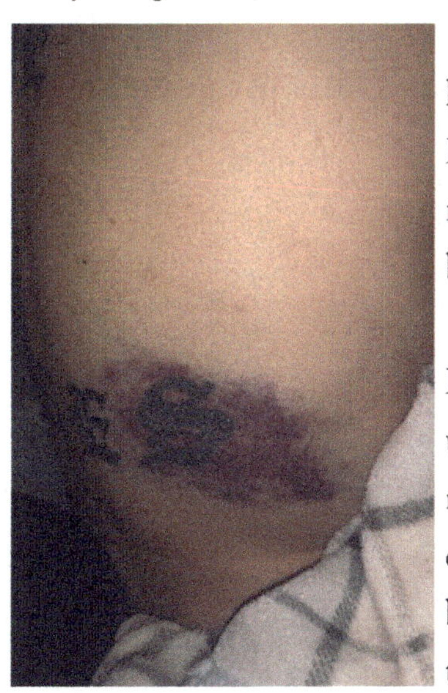

He left the hospital the next day to come home and immediately tried calling the Recovery Centre again...but again, there were no beds available and they said to try calling back the following Sunday.

At one point, when he took his shirt off, I noticed a huge bruise on his side. He never understood where it came from. He couldn't recall hurting himself in any way. Liver disease causes issues with bruising and bleeding easily because the liver is no longer able to produce the proteins needed for blood clotting.

Around that time, he'd been throwing up again. I sat on the bed and told him his fate was in his hands. He had honestly had so little alcohol, that it was hard for him to believe (and me for that matter) that it was what was causing him to get sick. He tried to say it was the food he'd eaten or that he'd had too much to eat. I reminded him he had eaten more than that on his birthday between the McDonald's and the cake, but he didn't throw up then. The dark cloud kept getting larger and I was starting to run out of hope that he would survive.

"I hope you actually believe me by now that my feelings are serious, and you don't think I'm lying," I said.

It's not that I thought he literally thought I was lying; it just seemed like he sometimes still had a lot of paranoia that I might cheat on him the way others had.

"I know you have strong feelings for me," he said as I started to lay down next to him. "I do too."

I don't think either of us ever really knew what to do with our situation. We lived and loved as long and hard as we could, but it was scary. Feeling so in love but having the stench of death breathing down your neck and hovering over you, is an odd and sad experience. I still question how I could be simultaneously so happy and yet so sad that we might get ripped apart eventually by something completely out of our control. We just wanted to be together...was that so much to ask?

The next day was a Saturday, and I was off work. Mark and I just cuddled on the couch under Yvonne's awesomely comfortable blanket. She was also at the house, but Jesse had gone downtown, most likely in front of Marie's. When he returned early in the evening, I looked up while I was lying on Mark's chest to see Barry walking in with Jesse.

Numerous times while leaving work to see Mark in the hospital, I'd asked Barry if he wanted to see him. He always seemed nervous about going or simply said no. So, it was nice to see them interacting again. He took a chair and sat near Mark's head.

"That's some girlfriend you've got there," he commented.

"I know, man," he responded in a disbelieving but grateful tone.

Barry grabbed a floppy hat that someone had given Jesse downtown a while ago and placed it on his head. He looked like how he sounded the night we were joking around and talking southern in the bedroom. Everyone found it hysterical. It's one of my favourite pictures of him.

Since Mark had last left the hospital, we'd come up with the idea of giving him very small mugs of White Russian every so many hours. I had also been reading a lot about my benzodiazepines and a phenomenon called "kindling." I had read about it years ago and then forgot about it.

It can happen with both benzos and alcohol. Basically, if you get off a substance that works on the GABA receptors like benzos and alcohol, getting back on it can make getting off that much harder the next time. The withdrawals can be worse when that happens. I wasn't sure if he knew about that. I think that also helped light a fire under his bum because we felt it might be why getting off the alcohol was so hard. He had quit briefly other times in the past.

I'm going to say right now just how proud I was (and still am) of Mark when he was doing this, especially as he was doing it without the Recovery Centre or the rehab, unlike other times. We got him down to having maybe three mugs a day filled with one cup of liquid. Half of that was milk, and the other half the vodka and Kahlua. That was a vast difference from drinking

40 oz. or more of vodka a day as he had in his past. He told me that over the months leading up to our getting together, he'd literally prayed to God for a kick in the pants to get well.

I was coming home from my new job around this time, feeling down in the dumps and like it was not working out very well. I felt like I couldn't do anything right and was paranoid I was going to be fired. Mark said he couldn't see that happening, but he was basing it on how he saw me working at Marie's. Don't get me wrong, I occasionally had these moments at Marie's too, but more than once, I told him I felt stupid.

"Don't say that. You're *not stupid*," he'd reply.

It was great he didn't think I was, but I still felt like I was failing and that the job wasn't going to last.

One night, we were going to sleep, and things got “affectionate.” Afterwards, he started to confide in me more about his first girlfriend...the one who really broke his heart. He told me how he'd burned all her pictures after he had caught her cheating with one of his best friends and how he was so broken-hearted. Mark had a way of bringing stuff up but being indirect about it in the past. As I said before, he’d been scared to leave me in town to go to rehab in Harbour Grace because of how previous girlfriends had cheated on him. It sometimes came up in little ways, but now he was getting more open about it, and we fell asleep talking. When we woke up, he sat on the corner of the bed, very vulnerable and back on to me. I was still lying down. He told me how strong his feelings were for me, without looking back.

"I don't like to talk about the lovey-dovey shit."

He was superstitious in more ways than just relationships and had made that clear in the past. "Don't say that!" he'd often say, thinking I'd jinx something and make it happen after I'd made some kind of comment. He reminded me of my mother in that respect. Shout out to Mom!

The fact that he found it hard to even look at me while talking about his feelings spoke volumes. Combined with the details he told me the night before, the picture was that much clearer of how scared he was of getting hurt. I have since read the whole story of what he'd written, and it makes so much more sense to me now. He had given me a hard copy in a binder to read in July, but so much was going on that I didn't have much time to read much of it. Jen and I had read the beginning (about his childhood) over the phone one evening, just before his seizure. When I finally got to reading it, I found out (as you already know) all those nasty details about how his ex didn't just cheat once; she did it repeatedly. I'm happy that he took the risk with me during the relationship and I was definitely not going to break his heart.

Those last few days he spent at home are a blur to me. Like I've said before, some stuff is hard for me to remember in exactly what order they happened. I have notes that I saved of most of it, not always intentionally. It's just because I had been writing about everything to my friend Jen over Facebook Messenger. Some stuff I kept notes about on my phone. There were some more minor things I'd forgotten.

Fall of 2021, I was cleaning out my fridge just before Christmas and found a fork in the pickled beets. It suddenly came back to me how many times I'd seen him chowing down on beets straight out of the jar. Not a bad idea for someone with a liver issue, as I've heard beets are good for the liver. Most stuff I've remembered, but the little things like that...I'm glad that they started to come back to me. My mind had been so stressed that the smaller things kind of got pushed aside for a while.

During these last few days at home, a few minor accidents occurred, including accidentally peeing his pajama pants. He hated that this stuff happened. I always brushed it off as I didn't care and didn't want him to get embarrassed about it. He was ill; it wasn't his fault.

I told him to go into the bedroom as I got a soapy cloth to clean him up. I went in and closed the door as Yvonne and Jesse (I was told) rushed to take the couch, which we usually took. I washed him up with the cloth and got him to put on a new pair of pajama pants. When I hugged him after, he got frisky again. He told me that my warmth against him when I hugged him felt "sexy." We started to kiss and fool around.

"I should pee myself more often," he joked (in those exact words).

Jesse and Yvonne couldn't contain their laughter when they overheard it. We still laugh about it to this day.

Anyhow, Mark was doing excellent at having minuscule amounts of alcohol. We were in the kitchen one evening and got to talking about it.

"I'm actually proud of myself," he said.

I told him that he should be and that he was doing so well. He had reached a point where he even went out for short walks a couple of times, and he seemed healthier than he had been in quite a while.

Then the incident happened.

We had been out of the vodka we were using for the whittling down of his alcohol consumption, and I told him I would pick up some on my lunch break. He legitimately forgot about this and asked Yvonne if she could pick some up. We ended up with too much vodka, as when I got home he already had a bottle.

The following day when I was going to work, I remember asking myself if I should take the extra bottle with me, just so the temptation wouldn't be there. But he had been doing so well that I didn't bother. That day he drank more vodka out of one of them than he'd had in a long time. I'm unsure if he made big glasses of White Russians or drank it straight. By the time I got home, I could tell he was drunk. I'd seen him that way while I was at work at Marie's for almost a year. I was so upset and worried, but I let it go and said we'd just start over again in the morning. He was still lucid, not blackout drunk, and could walk; but he was very much not his sober self. You could see the difference in his expressions. Penny had also dropped off a couple of laundry baskets full of his clothes that afternoon before he'd had his drinks. She also brought him his CD player and a cloth bag filled with all his important papers. Mark was slowly moving in and wanted more of his things.

He ended up craving bacon, but we didn't have any. I said I would walk with him to Halliday's Meat Market on Gower Street, and so we went for a stroll. He acted goofy the whole walk down Gower Street and while in the store. As we were leaving, I made some kind of a joke at his expense, and he said he was going to get me for it but couldn't keep the door open as he was trying to walk through.

"If I can even get through the door!" he laughed, fighting with it as he tried to follow me out.

Things got a little more serious as we neared the house again. He said he felt like he missed out on all the summer weather because of being stuck in hospital beds. He'd brought up going swimming multiple times, and he was disappointed that it was nearing the end of August, and he still hadn't even done that. He'd also wanted to teach me to swim.

We stayed up for a while after we got back, but eventually went to bed and everything seemed to be okay enough. He was slightly drunk, but he seemed fine. It was eleven or close to midnight when we went to bed. Two or three hours later, I woke up and heard him talking to himself in his sleep. I listened for a while as he kept saying the same thing repeatedly on a loop. I'd shake him, and he would just keep saying the same stuff. It was as if someone took a scene from a movie and looped it over and over. He was saying the same thing word for word every time.

I went out to the living room, and Jesse and Yvonne were still awake. I told them my concern and eventually called an ambulance again after neither Jesse nor myself could get Mark to respond. He reacted a tiny bit at one point; but other than that, he was saying the exact same thing over and over and seemed like he was stuck in a dream. I pulled up on one of his eyelids, which were open slightly, and his eyeballs were moving back and forth like in REM sleep. I found out this is called Roving Eye Movements and seems to be connected to hepatic encephalopathy. It's different from REM during sleep.

So again, I had to call an ambulance, and they took him to St. Clare's. When I arrived, he was hooked up to everything again and getting enemas with the lactulose. He just kept repeating stuff, and his eyes kept moving back and forth in a very mechanical-looking way. It would be over a day before I'd see him normal again.

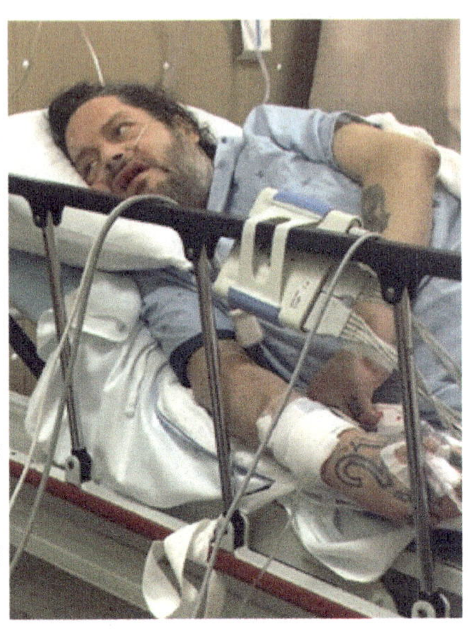

They eventually moved him from emergency and up to a room, where he continued to talk to himself. He even raised his fist in the air like he was mad at someone while lying on his bed. They had the radio on in the room, and he wasn't hooked up to any air or anything... he was just lying there talking to himself. I went up to try and talk to him at one point, and he swung at me and missed. I knew he wasn't conscious, so I didn't take it personally as he was delirious.

The day after that, it was the twenty-sixth of August; and I went in to see him and saw that he was standing up at the nurse's station in his hospital gown, looking normal. He watched me walk toward him down the hallway.

"Why the fuck did you call the ambulance? I was just passed out," he asked me as I got closer.

"Oh yeah? Wanna see the video?" I challenged him.

"Yeah!" he replied, sounding somewhat certain it would be nothing. We went into his room, and I played the three or four videos I'd taken for him.

"Wow! I don't look good...never mind," he laughed. "That's bad, dude!"

He started to bug the nurses to let him discharge himself since he felt normal now, and the hospital didn't want him to leave so quickly again. The doctor came to speak with him, trying to explain that they just wanted to keep him one more day, but he was determined.

The doctor didn't seem to consider it dire, so he just laughed at Mark and said okay. He prescribed him some antibiotics for the wet chest cough he'd had for a while, thinking maybe if there was an infection, it would clear it up. It always seemed to be there at a low level (worse at night) since he'd had the tube taken out of his throat from his liver stent procedure. I picked up his prescription for him from his pharmacy later that day. The doctor also instructed him to take the lactulose as often as he needed, not just two times a day as recommended on the label. He felt he should be good if he could get in three bowel movements a day.

Mark no longer had the Iron Maiden shirt I had just given him for his birthday. He'd been wearing it the night they took him in, and I believe they had to cut it off him and disposed of it. During this visit, they also lost his wallet, which he'd still had in his pants when he fell asleep at the house. I don't know if it's common for hospitals to lose belongings but they did many times. Luckily, it was just the debit card that he kept in there and no ID or anything like that. When he was leaving, they gave him a pair of scrubs.

Jesse and Yvonne went out that afternoon, and I sat with Mark for a while. He confessed to me that one of the reasons he always drank so much was because it made him more social.

"Seriously, I'm a shy motherfucker," he said.

It was so weird because to me, he was such a sweet, giving, loveable man. It just seemed like he couldn't see it in himself. He seemed to understand I loved him for him and that he didn't need alcohol with me. But to some extent, I guess he felt uncomfortable in his own skin...and, of course, old habits die hard.

Mark lay down on the couch while I started cleaning everything up, as it was much needed. I cleaned the living room as he relaxed and watched Netflix. He ended up falling asleep; and from time to time, when I needed a little rest myself, I'd climb in behind him and cuddle for a bit.

I got all his clothes that were brought over put away, and set up his radio on a set of drawers next to the dresser. Then I heard him throw up.

"Krista, can you help me?" I heard him call out.

I was confused about what he needed help with. I walked out and saw a splatter of bright red blood on the floor in front of the couch, along with some on the couch near his arm where he was lying down. I called an ambulance again. He'd only been home maybe five to seven hours, and he already had to go back to the hospital.

While waiting, I asked him if he would mind if I took a picture to document it in case it was needed or to show Yvonne and Jesse. He was fine with it. *If blood bothers you, please skip over the photo.*

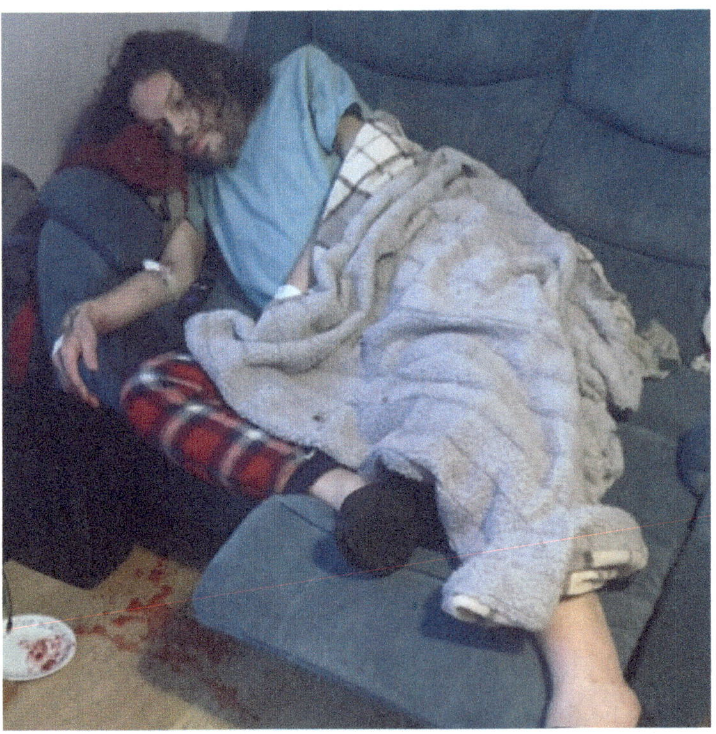

I share this stuff because if it helps **even one person to stop drinking and get help for addiction**, then it was worth it.

When the paramedics arrived, they asked him the usual questions and then he was able to walk out with them this time.

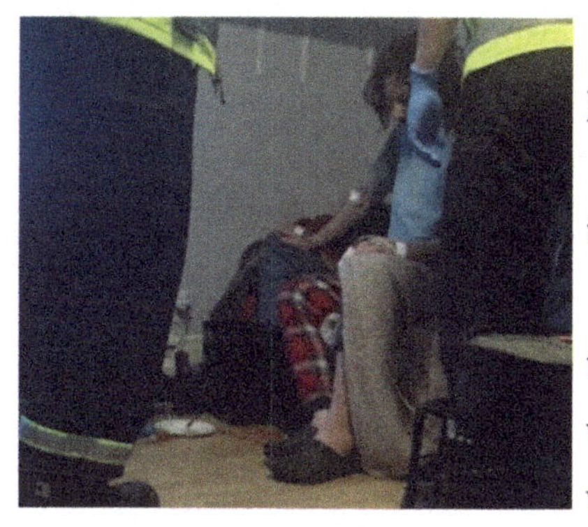

"I love you," I told him as he walked past.

"I love you, too," he replied sadly as they left.

I spent the next little while cleaning up the mess as I waited to make sure he was in the hospital, as usual. The blood wasn't just the bit on the floor; a third of the garbage can was full, as well. I called St. Clare's to see if he was inside, and they said yes. So, I got a cab and went to be with him. Jesse and Yvonne were confused when they got back, but I let them know what was going on...again.

The hospital told us he would get an endoscopy done in the morning and said he couldn't eat after midnight. But even though they'd told us that, they let him eat a sandwich and some chips after and claimed the endoscopy would just be done later. This turned out to be false. The next day they said they didn't find anything, but the food had been blocking a lot. I told the doctor that the nurses had said to go ahead and eat. It made me even angrier because it's even more dangerous should the person aspirate into their lungs during the procedure, which he did.

Neither the doctor nor I was happy about this mistake. I still don't know why they said it was okay. He ended up staying the whole weekend because they wanted to do another scope, this time with proper fasting beforehand. Before this, they gave him a blood transfusion. His hemoglobin was only 67g/L; for a man, it's supposed to be around 130-140g/L.

They moved him upstairs to a room, and he ate some chicken dinner with potato and broccoli. I swear I don't know how he did it. He often ate after being sick, including McDonald's, and it was no problem for him. I could never eat again so quickly after being sick, especially meat.

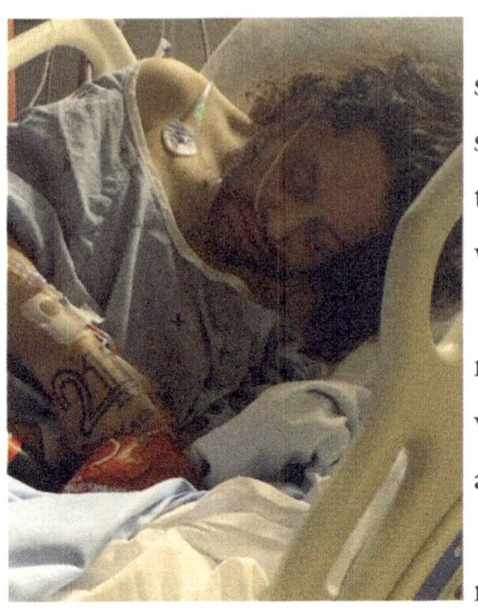

They eventually allowed me to get him some ketchup chips and soda. I wouldn't say that's the easiest on the stomach, but that's what he wanted. They told him it was fine.

Things seemed stable, at least for the moment. Mark got sleepy, so I left. Things went fine on Saturday, and all seemed to be all right when I went to sleep that night.

However, when I called on Sunday morning, they informed me that he'd thrown up litres of blood. The nurse told me it had been everywhere. They said they were so busy cleaning it all that they didn't get a chance to call me. I wasn't sure what to make of that because I thought that there would typically still be someone out at the desk. I didn't like this. He had thrown up litres of blood and I wasn't called right away. I was listed as his next of kin at this point. If anything is serious, I'd say throwing up blood is. I would have at least liked to have been given the choice to be at the hospital.

So anyway, I let it go and went in after they said it was all cleaned up. When Mark tried speaking to me, his voice was only slightly above a whisper. I figured his vocal folds were extremely irritated from throwing up all that blood.

After giving him another blood transfusion, they brought him down for his second endoscopy around half past four. This time, his hemoglobin went way down to 57g/L due to the incident in the morning. By about 6 pm, we were told that he had multiple spots bleeding in his stomach and esophagus and that it was a similar issue to the varices that bled back in June. They told us they used gas to cauterize it and stop the bleed, so there should be no more. Mark said it was the worst endoscopy he'd had so far, and he'd had a horrible one for the varices a couple of months before. He said that was a painful procedure for him.

He wasn't allowed to eat again yet, but he wanted to. Yvonne and I were meeting up and heading to Burger King. I asked him if he wanted me to

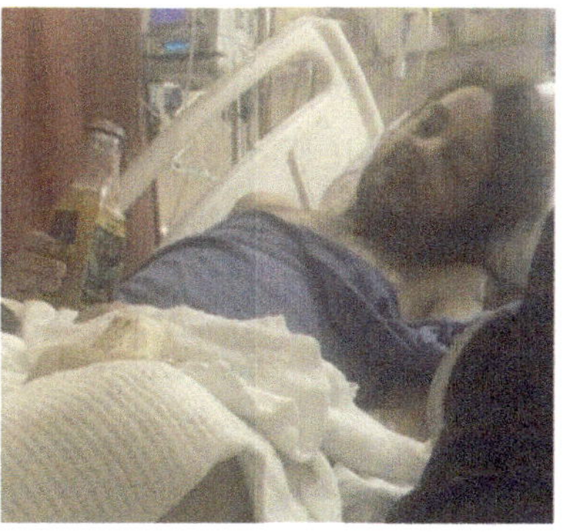

bring him back anything from any of the restaurants in the same area, as by the time I got back, he'd be allowed to eat again. I listed all of them off, and he said a wrap from Tim Hortons and an Iced Tea.

He was in a room with three other men during his stay this time, and while I was sitting next to Mark, I heard a familiar voice from outside the curtain. It turned out it was who I thought, another regular of mine from Marie's (though not a panhandler). I'm just going to call him Ted instead of his real name.

I found out for sure it was him as I was getting ready to take Mark out for a smoke.

"Are you trying to kill yourself, Mark?" he asked as he walked up to us while I was helping Mark into his wheelchair.

"Do you recognize me?" I asked.

He said yes, then told me he was in the hospital because he'd been diagnosed with lung cancer and only had a few months to live, which was why he was so obviously disapproving of Mark's smoking. He talked to us for a few minutes and returned to bed. He passed away in November 2021. It's very sad. He was always very nice to me. He came into work one day telling me he sometimes passed out these "Bell Let's Talk" hats for free. You can Google that if you don't already know what it is. One day, he came into the store with a couple for me. He was always very personable. I'll never forget running into him during Mark's stay in that room. Rest in peace, friend.

So at this point, they'd cauterized the bleeding...great! He was eating fine...great! When I left on Sunday night, things seemed fine and they had him on a clotting medication through his IV to help him heal up better.

He felt so much better that he told me he wanted to go home with me that night. I told him he should stay. I had him promise me that if he wanted to leave, he'd ask to call me and get my input first. He always left too soon, and I wanted to be sure that if he tried, I might be able to convince him to stay put. He had thrown up a lot of blood that morning. It would be suicide to leave the same day.

So, what did he do?

He came home the next day.

11 IF I DIE TOMORROW

Everything was okay when I had left the hospital the night before...I thought. As usual, Mark wanted to leave sooner than he should, so I wasn't overly shocked to get a phone call from the hospital upon waking up. I was going to head over and see him later, but he called and informed me he was calling a cab instead. He asked me if I could pay for it, as he had no money in his bank account right now, and I responded yes. I also told him he really shouldn't leave as he had thrown up so much blood the day before, not to mention they had him on clotting medication because he wasn't clotting well on his own. Before I could even finish trying to convince him, I heard the noise of the phone tapping something hard. It didn't sound angry, just like the phone had been laid down or lightly dropped.

"Hello?" I asked, confused.

All I could hear were voices in the background. To me, one sounded like Mark's doctor whom I'd met. No one checked to see if I was still on the phone; they just hung up. I called the hospital back in a rush and rang the nursing station, but when I talked to them, I was told he'd already left. The woman on the other end informed me that they tried to convince him to stay, but he refused and was due for more IV clotting medication.

Sometimes I wondered if he couldn't stay in the hospital because it felt like jail to him. I understand it can be boring there but he always seemed so anxious to leave, even if it was detrimental to his health. I was so upset and scared for him. Why didn't he keep his promise from the day before?

I went out to the living room to tell Jesse and Yvonne. I don't think either of them were particularly shocked, considering he always tried or did leave too early, for the most part. We were easily waiting for about an hour.

Between how long it sometimes took to get a cab since COVID had begun (a lot of people quit driving cabs at that time) and the fact that Mark always mixed up the name of our road with another road recently, it didn't shock me it took that long.

Eventually we heard a knock at the door (or kitchen window, I'm not sure), and no one was inside the porch when I answered it. I grabbed my credit card and headed out through the porch to the front door to find the cabby was standing on the sidewalk with her debit machine. Mark was sitting in the backseat with the door open, facing outward with both feet planted on the ground. He looked at me with those big blue puppy eyes as I walked over to the woman to pay.

"I'm mad at you," I said to him as I punched in my PIN.

His voice was still barely above a whisper as he told me that he'd explain. I thanked the cabby and helped Mark out of the back seat. He didn't find it too hard, and he was walking fine. I started to think maybe it would be all right somehow. He was kind of like a cat that way. They say when cats are sick, they hide it well, and Mark often did too. He seemed like a tank, especially since he could eat so easily after throwing up. Life could throw whatever it liked at him, but he was surviving it. As we were entering the porch, he tried to say that they didn't have much medication left to give him. He said he'd only have been in there probably another day or two.

We walked in and sat down. I was happy he was not in the hospital, but at the same time, I wanted him to stay there to get the proper help he needed. It came up about how it was Jesse's birthday, and Mark had lost track of the days because of the chaos. He said he was sorry he didn't have anything for him, but Jesse obviously understood with so much going on. He asked me to make him a small mug of White Russian. I told him I really didn't want him to do that because alcohol thins the blood, and he'd been on clotting medication, but he insisted.

"Can I use your cell phone? I want to try calling the Recovery Centre," he asked before I went into the kitchen. I grabbed my cell phone and called them before I mixed the drink, putting it on the speaker phone as usual. We were always doing this as it was just easier for him. I could hear tiny bits and pieces from the kitchen and when I came back in, he looked disappointed. The woman on the other end was telling him that there were no beds available and that they couldn't take him because he'd discharged himself from the hospital. If something serious were to happen to him there, they were not equipped to handle it. They needed to know he was well enough to go there.

Well, it would have been nice if he'd been told that one of the other times he'd called when they knew he had just left the hospital. Maybe he would have stayed put and waited to get discharged had he known. He looked a little defeated but figured they'd probably accept him eventually if he waited a while without anything terrible happening.

We sat and watched television for a bit and had a long talk about different things. Jesse and Yvonne were gone for a few hours and Mark eventually went to lay down. I heard him coughing at one point and asked him if he was all right. He spat into the black garbage can, and I grabbed a Q-tip to check what he'd hacked up. It was a tiny bit of light blood. I started to get upset, and he seemed a little nervous himself.

"It's only a little bit," he tried to reassure me.

I told him even a little is too much if he's coughing up blood. He disagreed, so I told him I'd give it a couple of hours to see what happened, even though I didn't want to.

Jesse and Yvonne came home, and Mark eventually came out of the bedroom. We hung out for a bit, then he decided he wanted to take a shower. He was in the shower for a long time. I almost want to say an hour, but it might have just felt longer than it was. It was at least thirty minutes before I heard some knocking on the sliding door to the bathroom.

Confused, I got up and peeked in only to find him sitting on the shower floor, unable to get up. The water was off, and it was extremely humid. A few bloody cotton swabs and bandages that had been on his body at the hospital were now on the shower floor. I tried to pull him up a few times, but nothing worked. Jesse asked what was going on, and when

I told him, he came in and tried the same thing, and again it didn't work. Mark looked exhausted, maybe a little embarrassed and frustrated, and he was wheezing badly.

"I'm going to slide in behind him, put my arms under his armpits, and try to pull him up that way." So, I wiggled in behind him. "As I pull up, you pull him out toward you," I told Jesse.

Luckily, that worked. We let Yvonne know that we were coming out with him, so she could avert her eyes, and we brought him into the bedroom. After we got him on the bed, Jesse left and closed the door behind him as I covered Mark up with our comforter. I lay down next to him and held him as he continued to wheeze. He was really struggling to breathe normally. I understood the feeling of taking a hot shower while already feeling weak. When I'd been sick a few years back, I found it hard even to take baths while weak. I was praying he'd find it easier soon.

He didn't say much but began to very slowly pull himself closer. He struggled, but eventually made it work and snuggled into my chest, wrapping his free arm around me with the humidity radiating off him. I stayed there with him, stroking his hair as he continued to strain to breathe normally. He had seemed relatively normal when he first got to the house, but this was a little scary to me.

"You know..." he quietly spoke up, "I didn't leave because I wanted to drink..." he paused, wheezing some more before continuing. "I left because I wanted to see you."

Even the way he said it felt romantic. He was very romantic or very foolish; I couldn't decide which.

Both, it was both.

I'd been so upset with him for leaving the hospital, but I was, and still am, so in love with him to this day. I couldn't help but love the stubborn mule that he was.

"But you could have seen me in the hospital. I was coming over later today," I replied.

"It's not the same," he protested, eyes still closed.

His words emanated with sadness and love as he said it. I already loved him so much, but it truly hit me in those moments how deep it went for the both of us. I'd known before, but I didn't know, if that makes any sense. Sometimes you think you know or believe something until something else happens, and you realize suddenly that you're more aware than you previously were.

The wheezing eventually calmed down, and I told him I would let him rest a bit. Later I heard him coughing yet again, this time harder. I opened the door, and he was still coughing. He was lying on his back, and before he could say anything to me, a quick spurt of blood came up over the side of his face, shoulder, and the bed. I immediately took charge and told him I was calling 911 again. No more of this, I knew he shouldn't have left.

After I called, I wiped him up, got his hoodie and pajama pants on, and slid his crocks onto his feet. They were the only shoes that could fit his swollen feet for a while now. He came out and sat down on this wooden chest I have in the living room, near the bedroom door and we talked with Yvonne and Jesse about everything.

"The nurses are going to look at me like I'm a fool," he said, sounding a little embarrassed.

"You keep leaving too soon," I replied. "So, stop leaving! If it will help you stay, and what you want is cuddles, I'll even climb in the hospital bed with you anytime you want it. You know that! We've done it before."

We went through the usual rundown of everything with the paramedics, symptoms and medications he was on etc. At this point, it felt like we were in the Bill Murray movie, *Groundhog Day*. We'd done the same thing so many times. He was able to walk out on his own again. We exchanged "I love you's," and he was on his way.

When I got to the hospital, he was awake and in bed. It wasn't long before he asked me to grab him the garbage can. I watched him sit up and vomit blood multiple times. It was another sight that still haunts my memory to this day. There wasn't much that could be done now, and his vitals were stable. My mind had been struggling with what to do about work. I had to work the next day, and I had to decide whether to call in and leave a message again. I'd called in so many times because of Mark ending up in the hospital in an emergency.

I didn't want to leave his side, but I had a bad feeling I was pushing things somehow, even though they'd told me to take the day off if he was sick. They were actually really understanding about it, but it had happened so many times at this point. I didn't want to risk losing my job, and no longer having the income to have a home to share when he got out. I'd explained this to him, and he completely understood. He had been sleeping for a couple of hours when I eventually left, and I didn't want to wake him. I still feel guilty about this to this day, even though we'd discussed it before he slept. I just wanted to be with him, but I was trying to keep my job *for us.*

I got up the following day and went to work. When I got there, I was asked if they could speak to me in their office. I immediately knew what it was. I didn't know for sure, but I had that feeling.

I went to sit down while the ladies began to talk to me about how business had not been as good as they thought it would be. I knew they were truthful on this, as everyone's hours had been cut back throughout the whole month of August. I was told they were going to have to lay me off (apparently, they were laying off someone else as well). One of them talked to me about Employment Insurance and how I'd be eligible for the higher amount that the government had offered for people during COVID. They encouraged me to get my info in as soon as possible as that amount would

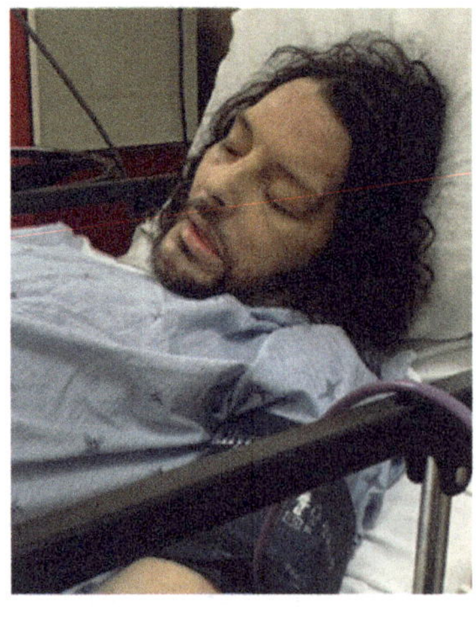

drop within a couple of weeks. They also told me to focus on being with Mark and to try and make sure I was taking care of myself as well while I was taking care of him. She became emotional as she knew him and his background. He'd told her how his problems had cost him a lot in his life.

"He's going to die knowing and feeling he was loved," she started to cry, and then I started to cry. "He's an amazing guy," she continued, "he just got caught up in some shitty stuff." She was spot on.

We continued to talk and I told them about how I met Mark when I went to work at Marie's, and how unexpected it was to fall in love with him. We talked about how I got to know him over the year or so I was there. We were laughing a bit, but then she said something I've never quite known how to take.

"First week and you're out on the sidewalk with him! There's a movie no one would watch."

Well, first off, as you've obviously read in this book, I wasn't out there with him the first week. She and the other ladies there all laughed at it though. It genuinely seemed to go over their heads perhaps, just how hurtful this sounded. It was said jokingly and with a smile. It hadn't registered right away for me, and I was still laughing at what they had been saying before she'd made this comment. Then it began to register in my mind, and my laughter began to feel uncomfortable.

What exactly did she mean by that? I don't know. I've tried to think of something else it could have meant other than an insult, but I don't know what else it could possibly be. I asked a couple of friends if I was weird for how it made me feel and they all told me they would feel weird too. Joke or not, to me, that's not a funny thing to say. Whether it was intended to be an insult...I have no idea, but I was hurt by it. Not only was I getting laid off, but to have to hear that?

I kind of wish now that I'd asked what she meant, but I was shaken up by everything that was going on and felt it might be too awkward. I've seen and talked to her on and off since, and I've never asked. I don't really care to. I've had multiple people tell me they thought it was pretty cool how we met. I forgive her for what she said. Maybe she just wasn't thinking; I don't know. I knew one thing, though: I was never telling Mark that comment. If it made me feel terrible, I was sure it would feel bad to him as well. I didn't want to chance that.

When I left my now-defunct job, I headed outside and saw Barry panhandling across the street next to Subway. I went over and talked to him about how I'd just been laid off, how Mark was doing, and what had happened. A couple of other locals asked me for updates as I stood there talking to him. I ran home with my papers and tried to apply for Employment Insurance.

That wasn't working out. I spoke for a bit to Jesse, who had still been on the couch when I got back (Yvonne was at work). I talked to him about what had happened and then headed back out to the hospital.

Mark was now in a room of his own within the ICU, unlike when I'd seen him in there before when he had his liver stent procedure.

His hemoglobin this time had gone down to 54 g/L. I was getting very scared. They had a tube going down through his nose this time, meant to suck the blood out of his stomach to try and keep him from throwing it up. I stayed there and talked with him for a while. I stood next to his bed and stroked his hair and his face.

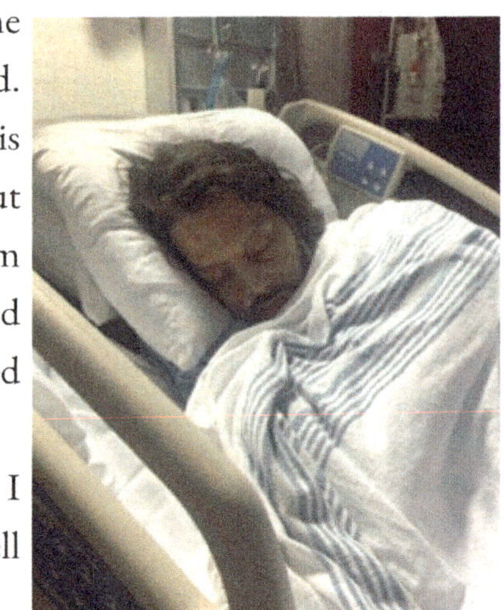

Finally, after some time had passed, I leaned on the bed railing and decided to tell him what had happened.

"So...I got laid off today."

He immediately shot me a stunned expression. "No!" he responded, sounding dumbfounded but still barely above a squeaky whisper. He was legitimately very shocked by this. I explained it to him without getting into the details of the hurtful comment that had been made.

"On the plus side...I can spend more time with you now," I continued.

Life can be so ironic and cruel.

I went in to see him the next couple of days, but was only ever allowed limited hours. That's the way the ICU was at that time. His doctor there told me they were amazed by him and said that Mark's kidneys, heart, and lungs all worked perfectly. Usually someone with a body that had gone through what his had gone through would not be working so well. I felt at the time that this was good news. Anyone would, right?

One day his social worker, Amy, was chatting with him when I got there. It was our first meeting in person. She sat on one side of the bed and I on the other.

"So, you told me about the 'cute girl from Marie's,' and here she is at your bedside. That's pretty cool. I mean...it's bad that you're sick."

Mark didn't say anything in reply. He looked to me as if he was looking at her kind of deadpan. I wasn't sure how to take it. It almost felt like: "Yeah...cool...but the situation sucks." Either that or, "Please don't embarrass me by talking about how I said that right in front of her." I can't decide which. Ha!

He asked Amy about getting new dentures and glasses so she could set that up for him. He'd had both before, but something had happened to them, and he'd not bothered to get new ones. I told him we both needed to start eating healthier too, and he agreed we would do that together. He also gave permission for Penny and me to continue to move his things from Garrison into my apartment. Our apartment. Penny said she'd be visiting him in hospital soon.

Mark really wanted to cuddle at one point when we were alone, so I asked his nurse if I could lie down with him. The nurse had someone help him adjust Mark in the bed to make room and ensure his tube wouldn't get pulled out by accident. I lay down with him and cuddled into him. From time to time, I glanced down at the nurse as he was sitting at his table. He was watching us almost contemplatively. It almost made me uncomfortable how much he watched, but I think he was taking it in. He knew how sick Mark was. Maybe he just thought it all looked really sad. I'm not sure, but that's how it seemed.

The third of September I took the bus up to St. Clare's. Mark had been moved up to a joint room, so I figured things were getting better. He'd had more transfusions, but that day they didn't want me to give him any food or drink. He'd been sick, and I was to give him nothing for fear he would throw it up. We talked for a while, and he began asking me for water. I had to keep telling him no and it was killing me more and more every time I had to say it. I told him the nurses said not to even give him water because it might trigger vomiting. He started to get very irritated with me, which was unusual except once or twice when he needed the lactulose. He tried to angrily raise his voice, but it still barely came out more than a squeak because of his vocal damage.

"Maybe you should leave," he said. "I don't like talking to you like this."

"I'm just trying to help you," I replied.

"I know, and I love you for it. I just can't hear 'no' right now."

We parted ways reluctantly for the day. Neither of us liked it, but he knew he needed time to cool off. He didn't really care if he gave the nurses a hard time in those moments, but he didn't want to hurt me in any way. I decided to walk home and made my way down Lemarchant Road and Long's Hill. I tried calling Penny to let her know he said to move the rest of his things. It was a Friday evening, so I never got an answer and just left her a voicemail.

He was exhausted and sleepy on Saturday. He was throwing up a lot, and his face was so gaunt at this point, especially around his eyes. They'd moved

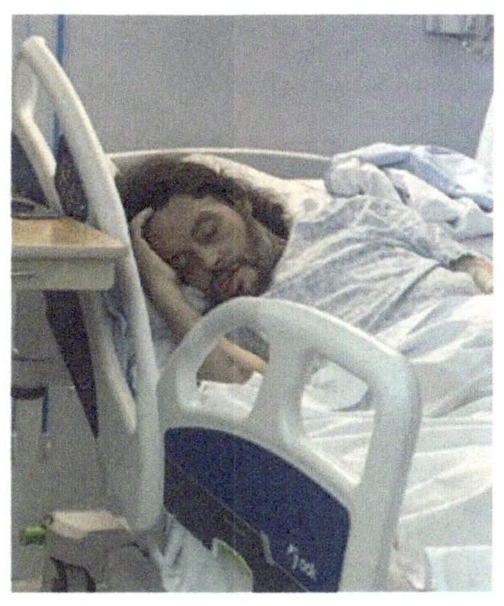

him to a private room, and he wasn't very talkative. He was exhausted by everything his body was going through. I just stayed with him, talking from time to time as he came in and out of consciousness. We never had to do anything big or talk much (though we often did). It was fine to just be.

Yvonne and I were meeting up to go for supper again as we had once before, so I left for a little while. We had our food and went to a nearby thrift shop before heading back. She pointed out a sign that said, "Never Give Up." I just felt sad but took a picture of it.

We walked back to St. Clare's and ran into my mom and stepdad, who were just getting back from out of town. We talked for a bit and then continued to the hospital. Yvonne headed back to the house from there. I went up to see Mark again and stayed with him for a short time, but he was zonking out even more now. I told him I was going to go home and get some rest and would be back the next day.

I went home around half past eight and had taken a much-needed nap when I got a phone call from the hospital around 11 pm.

The doctor told me they had talked to him about his condition and how sick he was and said there was really no hope of getting well at this point. So, she told me they explained to him about going on comfort care. My heart started to race at those words. No hope? Comfort care?

"She's going to be heartbroken," is what I was told he said when they spoke to him about it. He was also scared he was disappointing me. (*You could **never** disappoint me, Mark. I love you and you fought so hard.*)

I was not a fan of how the doctor spoke to me. She was very short with me, almost as if she blamed me for the fact that he was still alive. I had never pressured him in any way, he just didn't want to break my heart because he loved me. He'd told Yvonne he was trying to get as much time with me as possible. It had been his choice. He'd even gotten rid of his do-not-resuscitate order before this. He wanted to live, and he was fighting for more time. Why was that bad? Why was I spoken to so harshly? No bedside manner whatsoever, and that wasn't the last of it. Anyhow, I told her I was on my way.

I tried calling different cab companies, but everyone was telling me it was going to take a long time—especially as it was a Saturday night. So, in a panic, I got in touch with Mom, and she said she was coming to get me. Thank God she'd arrived back in town earlier that evening, otherwise I don't know what I would have done.

"I'm going to ask him to marry me," I told Jesse and Yvonne as I rushed to get ready to leave.

They both thought it was a great idea and that I should go for it. I should have just broken the ice about it after finding out how much he felt for me. I could have asked before then, but my own insecurities caused me not to do it. Plus, I really thought we had more time than we did. We both did. Mom came to pick me up, and we made a mad rush to the hospital.

12 LAST KISS

My feet couldn't get upstairs fast enough when I reached the hospital. I was even more irritated than usual by the COVID screening before being able to head to the elevator.

When I reached room 4165 on 4 West (yes, I kept track), the nurses left us alone to have some private time together. I got on the bed with him, unable to hold back my tears. We talked for a bit, and I figured we had a few hours at least. I went from sitting to pacing to sitting again. It was too much for me.

"We didn't get a chance to do everything we wanted to do," I said, muffled and crying into the nape of his neck.

"I know," he responded sadly.

I lay down finally and cuddled into him on the bed as he laid his head on mine. I felt him nuzzle my head every few minutes to get my attention for a kiss. He did this three or four times, and we said our I love you's. I was so distraught and none of it felt real. I wish I could remember every single last detail of it, but I was too beside myself and upset, knowing we didn't have much time left.

"Nobody's dying," he said at one point.

I questioned him about this as I was confused. Did he even know what he'd agreed to? He must have based on what we had said to each other so far. I think in hindsight, maybe he was trying to help me feel better in a weird way. It obviously didn't work. He just didn't want me to be upset. I kept going over things in my head and thinking of everything we'd wanted to do and never had the chance to. Mark was sounding so defeated at this point. You could tell he was exhausted in the worst way. Neither of us wanted to say goodbye to each other, but it was clear his soul couldn't take much more.

It wasn't long before the nurses came in with his medications. I'd only been there a short while, not very long at all. When I was about to get up, I knelt on the bed and gave him another kiss. As I pulled my face away from his, his eyes were still closed a few seconds longer. It gave me the feeling he was savouring it.

I moved out of the way for the nurses and stood near the wall at the foot of his bed. We looked at each other as they were prepping him for a shot (he no longer had an IV). He started to look like he was getting sleepy and drifted off while looking at me as they were getting everything ready. One nurse injected him with whatever comfort medication they were putting him on. He didn't open his eyes. I do know he was getting morphine and scopolamine. He'd said something about them offering him morphine when he was in the Health Sciences Centre after his seizure in July. He didn't want it because of his previous heroin addiction issues, as heroin is derived from it.

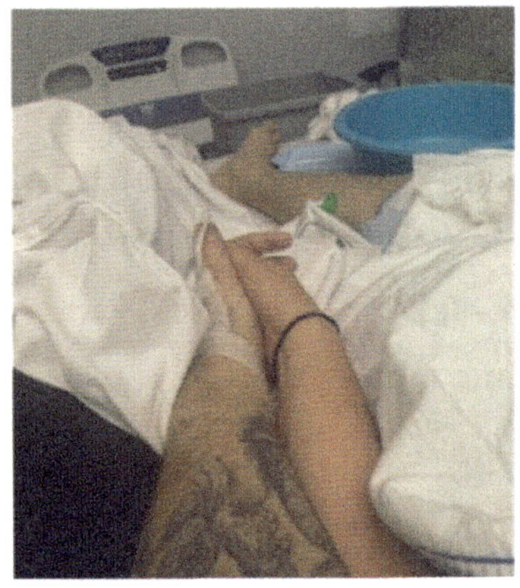

"Is he going to wake up again?" I asked nervously.

"Not sure."

I was even more upset now. I really thought we'd have more time together than we did.

"It's like he was holding on for you to get here," one spoke up, "to say goodbye."

They said that they saw that all the time. It didn't mean he wouldn't drift in and out of consciousness, just that they weren't sure.

I was so, so upset. I'd not been able to ask him to marry me. We didn't get much time at all. I don't think either of us realized how little time there would be. I've since found out through my mother that people often don't come out of sleep when they are on comfort care because of the medications. This angered me. It's like the nurses and doctor just assumed we'd both know, and we didn't. We would have requested more time together if we had known that. I know that 100%. Not just on my end, but on his as well; and I feel like those last moments were stolen from us in a sense.

Don't get me wrong, after my experiences in the hospitals I can genuinely say I believe nurses are human angels. They put up with and do a lot. They were fantastic. But I feel no one should have assumed that we knew that already, and it rips me apart to this day. I really was going to ask him to marry me. I know how he felt about me. I know in our hearts we were husband and wife to each other. We went through more together than some couples go through in thirty years. Some couples never get tested to the degree we had been with his health. I'd been told repeatedly, and still get told by people, that Mark wanted to and would have married me. I would have said yes had he asked. We were both so shy and insecure about it, and we honestly thought we'd get more time than we did, and I know God knows that.

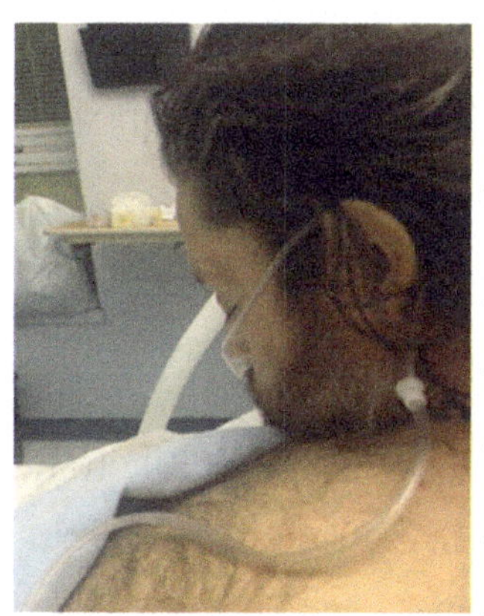

Something that I've heard of in some Christian circles is that God is not bound by his own sacraments and ordinances. Believers are supposed to do them, but that doesn't mean He is bound by them and cannot work outside of them. Going by that logic, and God knowing our hearts, I do believe He considered us to be married based on our intentions if we'd had the chance. I consider Mark my husband. I still say boyfriend and partner to people because many would be confused and it just takes too much to explain, so I'm doing it here. In my heart, he is my husband. I have no desire to ever be with another. I'm headed toward forty as I write this, and it took me thirty-seven and a half years to even *find him*. I'm not "giving up"; I just want to spend the rest of my life focused on other things now. He was it.

Recently, I'd reminded Jesse when he came to hang out at the house that I was going to ask Mark to marry me.

"Man, Mark TOTALLY would have married you. He wanted to. He loved you so much," he replied very loud and gruff with the biggest smile.

Anyone who knows Jesse well knows exactly what voice and expression

I'm describing. I will admit, I've been crying the whole time I've been writing this section of the book. By the time I complete the book, it will be a year later, and I'm still hurting so much.

Not long after Mark went unconscious, he began vomiting. This was another one of the most horrific things I've seen in my life. It's kind of gross, but as I've said previously, I include all the details because if it helps even one person get clean, it's worth it.

He was unconscious, and the vomit was just spurting out of his mouth...almost projectile. They put his bed up so he wouldn't choke. He wasn't moving or reacting. It was like watching a mannequin spew it, but it only came out in spurts. They had on protective garments and were holding the "puke tub" to try and get it because it was so unpredictable. How did I go from being phobic of this stuff to watching this?

"Do you think he's done?" one asked the other after he'd stopped for a bit.

I think he may have thrown up a couple more times after that, and then it just...stopped. Everything stopped.

They cleaned him up, as well as anything else that needed cleaning. His hospital bracelet was removed and placed on his table next to his cell phone, and so started the process of about thirty-six hours of lying with him. I didn't leave his side during the process, and I only left to pee. Even then, I told him I was only going to pee and would come back immediately in case he could hear me. Mark was terrified of death and I wanted to be sure he knew I'd not left him for long.

The first night was brutal. I was on constant high alert in case he passed right away, but the reality is sometimes it can take days. The nurses came in to shift him in the bed from one side to another every few hours, check the diaper they had on him, etc. Once or twice during that time I was crying so painfully that I'd asked Mark to take me with him...and I truly meant it. I don't have the guts to ever go through with suicide, but...I meant it. I wanted God to let us go together. Just, poof, gone.

At some point during the night, I found myself singing to him quietly—very quietly like a lullaby. I didn't want the nurses to hear it. I can't remember every song, but I did sing *Can't Help Falling in Love* by Elvis...because it was true. I sang *Anywhere* by Evanescence, a song I strongly associated with us. I know there was more than that, but as I said, I can't remember them all. I didn't do a whole lot, but I just felt that urge to sing to him. I got maybe a couple of hours of sleep, total, lying next to him. I didn't want to risk being asleep when he died, and my body hated me for it. I'd nod off a bit, then wake up again, over and over. Nurses often asked me if I wanted anything to eat. I usually just had dry toast, and from time to time I was able to eat a bit of cheese and drink milk. Truthfully, I think the milk kept me going much better than I would have been without it. I could barely stomach anything because I was too upset.

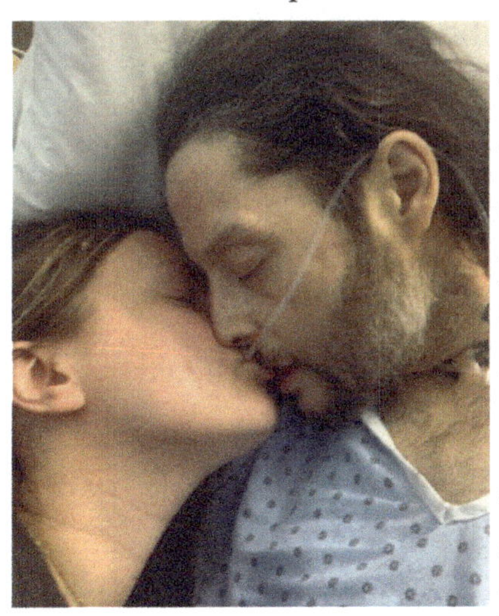

I became very sweaty and gross while being glued to him. Many would perhaps think that someone's body would feel cooler as they are dying due to the body processes shutting down, but he was hot to the touch. I didn't care; I just wanted to hold him.

The next day, Sunday, Barry and Suzie showed up to visit. Suzie got angry again as she had at the Health Sciences Centre. I won't go into the details of it, but she was distraught and kept telling Mark to get up. Barry again brought up how Mark wanted to marry me.

All I could think of when he said it again was how I knew he did, yet here we were...not officially married because everything was rushed on us. Most of the conversation I had with them is a blur because I was so stressed out and exhausted from a lack of sleep. Suzie left to go downstairs for a smoke and eventually Barry went with her. He said he'd be back, but neither of them returned. Later I found out someone called the cops because Suzie was unruly and upset, and they ended up both getting taken away. Everyone was very upset and expressed that in different ways.

Later, my mom came down to visit. She'd only seen Mark in person from the car in the past. They'd never spoken, and as I said before, she'd been leery of the whole thing because of my last relationship. I think she regrets it now, but that's all that can be done. It meant so much to me that Mom came and talked to me while he was still breathing. I have faith he knew she was there. She told me the fluid sound on his chest as he breathed (known as the "death rattle") was the same way Grandpa was as he was dying. It was a very bittersweet moment to have Mark and my mother in the room at the same time under those circumstances...but I'm glad she came.

At some point (I can't remember if it was that night or the night that he first went unconscious), a nurse asked me if I'd like for a chaplain to come in, talk, and say a prayer. I knew Mark never seemed to turn down a prayer. I knew he had felt sorry for the things he'd done in his life, so I figured a prayer would be welcomed. The chaplain was a priest. I'm not sure if he was Catholic or Anglican now, but he was very nice. He talked to me for a bit about us and then prayed for us—both for Mark's passing to be peaceful and for my emotional well-being in the process and afterward. I really appreciated it.

In the middle of the night, early on the morning of the sixth of September, Jesse and Yvonne finally came to the hospital for a few hours. I'd asked Yvonne to bring me a change of shirt, underwear, and socks so I didn't feel so gross. When they got there, we chatted, and Jesse spoke to Mark. We all just hung out together for the final time.

Jesse called his brother Justin whom I mentioned earlier had known Mark before him. He wanted to be put on speaker phone so I held the phone near Mark; and Justin stated that he didn't know if he could hear what he was saying, but he wanted him to know it wasn't too late. Mark had feared hell, and Justin had become a believer himself, as I stated earlier, so he decided to give him the Gospel.

I'm pretty sure Mark knew it anyhow, but you never know. Justin wanted to be sure he heard it. He told him that Christ had died for him and for anything he had done wrong. He reminded him that if he was truly repentant (which he was...that I knew) and turned to God, he could still be saved.

None of us took offence, though we were not Christians at the time. Mark wouldn't have either; that was clear from our conversations. Justin then prayed with us over the phone, and Jesse thanked him as we said goodbye, and Justin said goodbye to Mark. This conversation had a significant impact on me, and I have faith that he heard it. They decided to return to the apartment instead of sticking around and said their goodbyes to Mark.

"Hey, Yvonne? Take one last picture," Jesse piped up before they left. It's so incredibly heartwrenching for me to look at. The love and pain by turns is intense. I can still remember the feel of his face and body against mine in that bed.

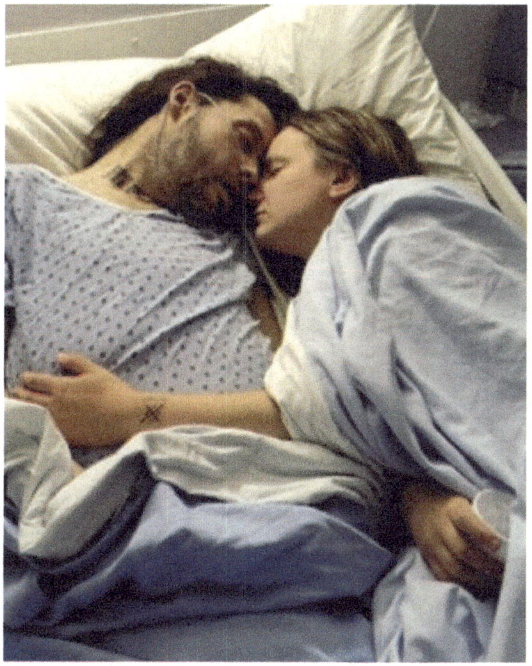

After they were gone, I fell asleep for a few hours beside him. I guess my body just couldn't fight the lack of sleep anymore. When I woke up it was completely light outside. It was Labour Day morning. Almost the whole time we'd been lying together, I kept praying to God to please just allow me to see his blue eyes one more time. I had thought about it so many times over those last thirty-six hours or so.

I continued to speak to him as I had been the whole time. I was telling him how as a child, my grandpa took me for walks on the waterfront and on Harbour Drive. We'd walk along the wharf. I told him now, that any time I walk down Water Street, I'll think of him because it's where we met. I'd initially stated elsewhere that I felt this was about twenty minutes before he passed, but I'm not positive about that as time moved weirdly for me during this whole process.

"It's ten to 11 am," I told him, then paused, feeling dumb. "I'm not sure why I just told you that." I ended up propping myself up, and I looked over at him, and **his eyes were open**!

I was a little bit excited for a moment, and I told him I'd been praying to see his blue eyes again and asked if he could speak. There was no sound other than his breathing which was getting slower and slower now. I suddenly realized I'd had a moment of false hope that he would somehow cheat death again.

Every time he took a breath, it was almost mechanical sounding because of the air they had him on. It's hard to explain. His eyes were on me. With every breath, there was a more extended period in between. There were a couple of times I thought he was gone, but another breath would come. Until finally...no...more.

I started to panic as I looked at the tears that had formed in the corners of his eyes just as he died, magnifying the blue. I felt his chest, and I couldn't feel his heartbeat. Everything felt very still.

I used the buzzer on the bed to get a nurse to come in, and she immediately confirmed he was gone. She turned off the air and removed the nasal cannula, telling me I could have as long as I needed with him. She asked if I wanted them to call anyone, so I told her to call my mother as she was just up the road from the hospital. She got her number and left me alone with him. I just kept crying and looking into his eyes. I don't think he could actually see me when he passed away, but his eyes were on me, and that gives me such mixed emotions. I had prayed to God to see his eyes one last time, and I did. Since then, I've found out some people's eyes do open in the final moments before death due to something about the process. So, I'm sure many will say it was not a miracle, but it only happens with a smaller fraction of people, so it was a personal miracle for me.

It occurred to me later, with him being adopted, there was no one in his life currently who had been present when he entered the world. I was the one person with him when he left it. To say that realization hit me hard is an understatement. It was a sacred moment, and I was holding him. Knowing him, he probably wanted it that way.

Mom arrived and told me later that the sight of me clinging to his dead body was one of the saddest things she'd ever seen.

"It's just his body. Remember that," she said, softly.

She said that to remind me that the soul goes on.

We had to wait for the doctor to come to talk to me. I got off the bed after Mark's face started getting cold. I didn't want to remember him cold. I put on the black hoodie he'd worn when he last came to the hospital on Jesse's birthday, sat with Mom, and talked while we waited for the doctor.

When she arrived, she was very to the point and rude, just like she had been on the phone with me before. She told me how I'm still young (I look much younger than I am) and can now put this all behind me. She began saying I should go back to school. I honestly wanted to clock her. I told her that I was thirty-eight years old, had done school, and had just been laid off from my job. It was insulting. Worst of all, it felt like a slap in the face to Mark. It felt like one last slap of indignity and disrespect. She was judging me and making assumptions about me, my life, and my character. As a result, she was also judging Mark.

Do you honestly think she would have said such a thing if, perhaps, he'd been an MHA like my dad was? Of course not! You'd have to be pretty naive to believe that. I've been working on forgiveness in my life. I'm still finding it hard to forgive her, both for what she said right after Mark died and how she had spoken to me over the phone. It was awful to be sitting there, hearing her say these things with Mark's dead body right behind her. I kept looking at him as she spewed her garbage. It was completely disrespectful. I'd call the hospital to find out her name and talk to her at some point to voice my distaste, but many doctors that I've had experiences with have had a God complex and enormous egos. Not all, but many. I know she wouldn't give a care in the world what I had to say to her anyhow. It's just something I'll have to work on.

I told them which funeral home to send his body to for cremation, and then it was time to go. I gathered his belongings, including his last hospital bracelet, which I still have. We slowly began to walk toward the door to leave, and then I looked back at him in the bed. His beautiful blue eyes had been closed now, and they had the sheet up under his chin. He just looked like he had fallen asleep with his mouth open like had happened so many times at home. I told Mom to hold on one second, as I had one more thing I just knew I had to do or I'd regret it.

I slowly walked over, staring at him the whole way, and then looked down at him alone in the bed. After a life of almost constant struggle, he looked peaceful.

This was the last time I'd see him. It killed me inside, and I'm crying even as I'm typing this. It felt like it happened in slow-mo. I bent over and kissed his lips one last time. I remember really taking it in so I would never forget it. They were cold, but I didn't care anymore. This was the last chance I'd ever have to touch the man I loved more than any who came before him. He was taking a part of my heart with him. I couldn't say goodbye without that one last kiss.

13 ONE DAY

Mom was driving me home after leaving the hospital, so I told her to go down to Water Street. I didn't know if Jesse would be at the house or in front of Marie's. Jesse wasn't there when we arrived, but Barry was. I asked her if she could let me get out for a few minutes to tell him and swing back around. I got out of the car, and as soon as Barry saw me walking toward him in Mark's oversized hoodie, he knew.

"Nope," he said as he began to get up and walk away from me. "Nope," he kept saying. He stopped, and I hugged him and told him he was gone. "Fuck!" he kept saying in disbelief.

Mom was coming around, and I told him she was driving me back up to the house, so he hopped in her back seat and came up with me. Mom dropped us off outside another nearby convenience store, Caine's. They have home-cooked meals. I was literally starving at this point despite being very upset, so I grabbed a Turkey Jiggs dinner. Barry picked up a pack of Molson XXX and we walked back to the house from there. He told me that he wanted to tell Jesse himself.

When we entered the living room, no words even needed to be said. Jesse got up and walked toward us. He grabbed Barry in a tight, tearful hug and pulled me in. Yvonne joined in too. We were all hurting. Our family was broken now.

They cracked open the beer, and I was so upset that even I had one. I don't typically drink except for some wine or Kahlua. I'd had other drinks, but I was never one for getting drunk, especially with my phobia of getting sick... but especially not on beer! You'd think due to Mark dying that morning, I wouldn't have touched alcohol, but I was so beside myself that I had one.

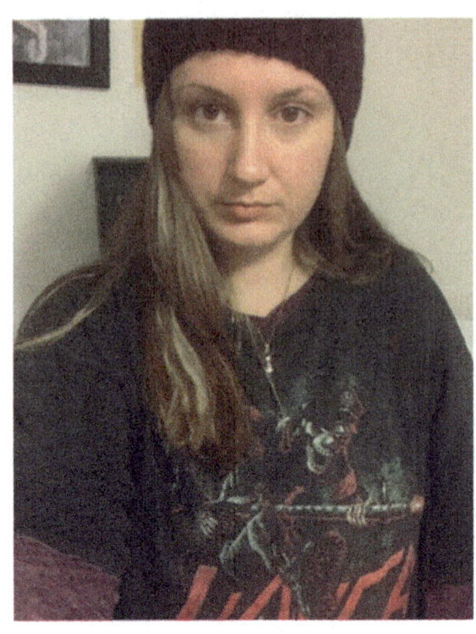

"Fuck it! Give me one!"

I've never drank beer as fast as I did that one, since I never found the taste of beer pleasant.

I warmed up my dinner and gravy and ate almost all of it. We hung out and watched YouTube on my Roku for the next little while, just like Mark, Jesse, and I had done months before. We took turns putting on music that reminded us of him. I put on *Anywhere* and *My Immortal* by Evanescence, with the former being one that I sang to him in his hospital bed. I also chose *I'll Follow You into the Dark* by Death Cab for Cutie, which I would later quote from in his obituary when I wrote it. Another song, *Downtown*, by Majical Cloudz, was from the Netflix show, The OA. It appears in a particularly poignant scene, and the lyrics definitely suited us. One song that will always stick with me from that day is *Wake Me Up When September End*s by Green day. Of course, we also put on Pink Floyd, Manowar, and Mötley Crüe. There were so many songs, and all dedicated to Mark.

We decided to eventually go out for a walk. I went into my bedroom and got changed. I put on the Slayer shirt I'd seen him wear so many times, a long-sleeved shirt underneath, and my hat. We all went for a walk down Water Street.

"Mark would have thought you look wicked cool right now," Barry piped up.

We made it back down to the area of Marie's. I'd messaged my mom where I was, as she was supposed to pick me up to go to the funeral home to discuss stuff with them. I picked out a little urn for some of my lot of ashes and a necklace that says, "Always in my heart," which would have some ashes in it as well. I've worn it every day since I picked it up and have only taken it off to shower. I gave them a rough number of how many containers

I would need of ashes, as he'd told me he wanted any friends that wanted some to get some. I sent some off to friends of his who live on the mainland, and some went to friends here. I got a few more containers later before they shipped the rest off to his parents. He wanted the rest of them scattered on his grammy and grampy's graves. His family also put some on the train tracks back home. It was suiting for Mark as he had enjoyed train-hopping all those years. I thought it was a nice choice on their part.

I kept a few containers for myself and I've spread them in different areas around town, most of it is from one container. You don't really need much. The rest of the containers I've kept for myself. I've put in my will that when I die and am cremated as well, all of his ashes that I have are to be put in the urn with mine. At least, after my friends get any ashes of mine should they want any. I know a few who do. I also want him on my tombstone with me. It sounds morbid to talk about, but we all will die someday. There's no point in sticking my head in the sand. These meat sacs are temporary. To dust, we will return.

It didn't take too long at the funeral home, maybe a half-hour, then Mom dropped me off downtown again. I sat with Jesse, Barry, and Yvonne at one of the usual spots, right next to Subway. From there, I typed up a long Facebook post about Mark's death using my data. He probably never dreamed in a million years that the girl he met at Marie's, just across the street from there, would be sitting outside with his friends, writing a post about being with him as he passed away. It felt so strange sitting there doing that. I had such an overwhelming reaction to that post. The news spread amongst downtown locals like wildfire. I had people messaging me and telling me they were sorry for my loss, not only from Newfoundland, but all over. So many commented on other people's sharing of my post and expressed condolences or said they thought we had a beautiful bond, etc.

A few comments did drive me a little nuts, like comments to do with the alcohol abuse. Some talk about him as if all he was, was a drunk and drug addict. Others kind of gave a wink and a nod to him by getting plastered themselves. He knew why he was dying and wasn't okay with it. He told me he wanted to do his life over. I so wish people would think twice in that respect.

All three friends slept in my living room that night, but I opted to stay alone in my bedroom. The nights would continue to be hard on me for a very long time. They sometimes still are. Those first couple of months were ruthless for me and I went to sleep crying often. I've never in my life, under any other circumstance or from any other death, had this much of a hole-in-the-chest feeling. It really hits differently when it's a romantic partner, and he was so much younger than everyone else I knew who had died within my family. I'd had a couple of friends die, but it didn't cause the same kind of agony. I call it a black hole, which is honestly as good as the description is probably going to get. It scared me...it scared me enough that I started going to grief counselling. I continued to get counselling not only for the grief I felt over Mark but for Dad and some of the other things I've been through in my life as well. It's been a roller-coaster ride. The sessions with that counsellor were done at the end of June 2022 and as of writing this, I'm on a waiting list to start a special trauma program. It was recommended to help me learn to cope with a lot of my PTSD from various things in life, including some of the things I witnessed when Mark was sick.

The house was empty when I got up the next day, and everyone had left. I decided to put on one of Mark's CDs and flipped through his CD booklet. He had Johnny Cash in there, though strangely I didn't put that on. I decided to put on Mötley Crüe. I wasn't expecting the song that came on towards the end. It was called *If I Die Tomorrow.* I'd never heard it before, and the whole thing felt so much like Mark and me. I could have put on any number of CDs to blast that day, and that was the one that I picked. The song couldn't have been more perfect for what had just happened. I truly believe I was led to play it.

A couple of days later, I talked to Penny and headed to Garrison Place to clean out the rest of his stuff from his apartment. It felt bizarre because he'd been in the process of moving in, and it all would have been moved soon anyhow. It just felt like I was in the wrong universe. All I could think of was that we should have been doing it together. If I hadn't used my common sense, I would have taken everything with me, but he had some stuff like hockey equipment that someone else could actually get some use out of. I did take most of it though, including his guitar. The rest they donated.

I've since sold the shiny new guitar I'd financed from Long & McQuade a couple of years ago, as I now only play his. It helps me feel closer to him.

We ended up having his Celebration of Life at a bar Mark frequented on George Street. The owner had helped him out a lot and used to let him sleep in the bar before Mark had an apartment. He trusted him completely, and he never stole a thing or caused him any trouble. He was there for Mark and, since he used to be a nurse, even helped him understand his test results when he got diagnosed. One day I walked down to discuss the memorial with him in his office.

"Those last weeks Mark was alive were probably the happiest of his life even though he was so sick," he told me.

I would later find out when Yvonne and I went to see him in December, that Mark had told him earlier that year that he really had a thing for the "girl from Marie's." It feels like *so many* people knew before I did. It boggles my mind a bit that I was so clueless to it.

When I'd gone through Mark's apartment, I found a lot of coins from different areas of the world that he must have collected while panhandling. All

of them were foreign currencies from countries he'd never even been to. I bought a little gold pirate chest to keep them in since we shared a love of pirates. I keep calling him Captain Cambers, and I, Lady Cambers.

Arr! Ye wench be looking after yer treasure, Captain!

Near the end of September, Yvonne and I went for a stroll downtown and ran into Jesse unexpectedly. He'd been at the Recovery Centre and just got out earlier that day. We decided to go for a walk and headed up to Signal Hill for a hike. It was a beautiful, sunny day, and it felt like Mark was there with us.

Jesse jumped in the ocean at two different points, once in Cuckold's Cove and the other in Quidi Vidi Gut, where he swam over to the other side and stupidly (yeah, I said it!) tried to climb the rock wall. Of course, he only got up so far.

That first month after Mark passed was tough, and it felt like we all got our first breath of fresh air since it had happened.

Both Yvonne and Jesse were still around a lot throughout the last bit of 2021. I needed that company, but on some level, the real healing began when it was just Lumi and me again. I was then alone more to process everything.

I had the idea to take Mark's last name as my own because we never got to get married. I wasn't sure at first, for reasons outside of myself. I knew our friends would get it, but I was thinking of others who really should have no say in the matter and who didn't truly know us as a couple.

A friend of mine that I used to work with had driven me to pick up his ashes from the funeral home, and as we were sitting there, she asked me what his last name had been, so I told her.

"Krista Cambers," she said thoughtfully. "Have you ever considered pulling a Rose Dawson?"

The fact she referenced *Titanic* amused me because, as you already know, the movie had come up.

Well, I'm now legally Krista Cambers as of November 2021! Everyone thought it was great and knew Mark would have loved it. When I got my new name change certificate and birth certificate, I showed them to Jesse and Yvonne. I was so excited and they both thought it was awesome.

"Hey, Krista?" Jesse asked a while later out of nowhere.

"Yeah?"

"It does have a nice ring to it."

"Krista Cambers?" I asked.

"Yeah...I dig it," he said with a cheeky grin.

Jesse and Yvonne have continued to be family to me, and both have their own apartments now. That was something Mark wanted for Jesse...to have a stable home base and to clean his life up. He didn't want him to go down the same road he did in life.

Christmas was especially hard for me. I had some empty nest syndrome even though I'm not a mom. It was just very quiet. Like I said, this was when the actual healing process began—both about my grief and having issues trying to cut down my anxiety medication.

I watched *Christmas Eve on Sesame Street* late on Christmas Eve, like Mark had wanted to do with me. There were a few times mail came to the house from Eastern Health addressed to him. For one reason or another, he still had a couple of appointments I needed to cancel. It was all very strange.

I was so scared of ending up like Rose in *Titanic* (like I'd told him), yet here I am, doing all those things we talked about or that help me feel close to him. It's sadly just like I'd feared. It is what it is.

I could be really angry with God for bringing Mark into my life only to take him away. But since he passed away, I've had my fair share of very extreme, weird experiences that I refuse to go into detail about except with those closest to me. Those that know...know. Experiences weird enough that I'll say it must be by the power of God at this point. All I will say is that when Mark was alive...he was so sorry and scared that God would never accept him, but I've had enough experiences that I believe he is okay. I could even put the word "know" in there.

I had friends, firm believers in God, who even questioned why God "did this" to me, but He always has a bigger plan in mind, and they understand that now. Mark was a part of His plan for me. What I've experienced has been enough that I was adamantly against Christianity for many years, but I came back as a result of my experiences. Believe me that this would not be an easy task, and I still pinch myself that I've even done it.

The lapsed Salvation Army girl fell in love with the alcoholic street kid. For those who don't know, William Booth, the founder of the Salvation Army, was a Methodist minister who wanted to help the poor, needy, homeless, and addicts. It started as a movement, not as a church.

The irony has never been lost on me. What were the odds I'd fall in love with someone who lived most of his life on the streets? And that he, of all people, was how I was led back? Not specifically to the Salvation Army but to Christianity. I was never anti-alcohol. I know most can drink it in moderation, but after seeing the condition Mark had himself in and knowing others who are addicted to it, I can understand something my grandfather used to say.

"If you never take that first drink, you can't become an alcoholic."

Sounds strict, right? He was a Salvationist after all, but I understand it so much better now.

I've now cried my own tears over the things I've done or could have done better in my life, but just like Mark, I know I'll be okay. I don't expect everyone to believe me, but we can agree to disagree. I'm not going to shove my beliefs down your throat...they're just mine. I'm open to discussion, but I'm not going to hate on you. That's not my style.

I know Mark and I met for a reason. In reality, probably many reasons. I genuinely believe that he is my true love and always will be. Our time here is a temporary thing, and I want Mark to be the first face I see when my time comes, when I truly wake up and I'm called home by God.

I titled this final chapter *One Day*, after the Hans Zimmer music from the third *Pirates of the Caribbean* film. It plays as the characters Will and Elizabeth have to part ways because he's taken over the ship, the Flying Dutchman. As a result of a series of unfortunate events, he can only step on land one day every ten years. So, they have their one day before he heads back out to sea, and the longing in the scene is brutal. We, too, are separated...for a time. I hope you've learned or felt something from our story. As I've said, if it helps even one person, it's worth it. So thank you for sharing in it with me. I'd seen and heard it said so many times by the older generations in my family regarding passing away:

"We will meet again in the morning."

They spoke of a different morning than any of us have experienced yet, but I feel he will be there in that morning waiting for me.

With that, I want to end this with a few simple words for Mark...

You've profoundly impacted me in many ways and showed me so much about this world and myself just by you being you. You showed me how unfair the world can be to people who are suffering (on multiple levels), but you also showed me how beautiful a heart someone can still have, even after being knocked down by so much. People judged you because you had addictions, made mistakes, or because you sat on the sidewalk, but you were no hypocrite like so many that are out there.

You were as real as someone could get, and you had what truly matters in this world and the only thing you can take with you. Love. You were a good man who got caught up in some nasty stuff. When I talked to you about God's forgiveness, you indirectly got me to remind myself that it's never too late for anyone when it comes to this world or the next. You once said I could do so much better than you, but the reality is, for me, there is no one better. You were one of a kind. ***I love you, Mark, and I always will.***

Signed,
With *love and many kisses,*
Your *"cute girl from Marie's"*

Above: A couple pictures of Mark during his early years on the street.
Below: Mark in his dentures showing off a big toothy smile down at Harbourside Park when Jesse first visited.

Below: Pictures from when Jesse first brought Yvonne to the province for a visit in 2019.

Above left: Just after Jesse had arrived in town in spring 2021. I can tell Mark is hammered there.

Above Right: Various bottles of vodka and Kahlua on Mark's table at Garrison Place.

Above: Another picture I'd taken of Mark and Jesse outside Marie's. This was the day after he'd left the hospital after having his liver stent procedure.

A tale of a kitty and her boys. Lumi keeping Mark company when he wasn't feeling great. This was during the first week they stayed at the apartment. And another snuggling with Uncle Jesse on the floor (yes, I use that term with her).

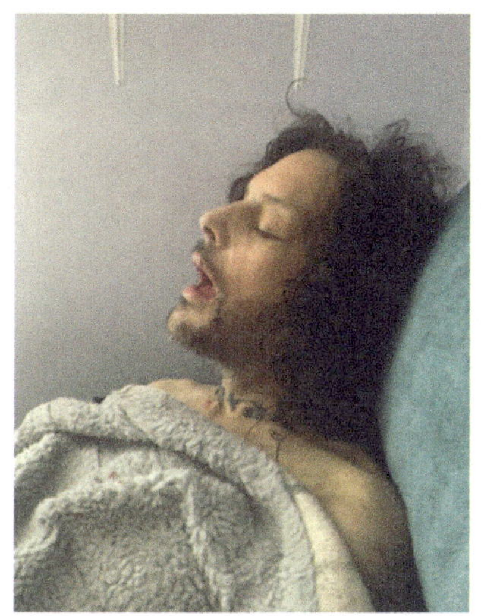

Above left: Mark passing out on the couch.
Above right: Me wearing Mark's infamous overalls after he'd passed.

Above: Yvonne and I, December 2021 downtown on Water Street. Marie's is in the background.

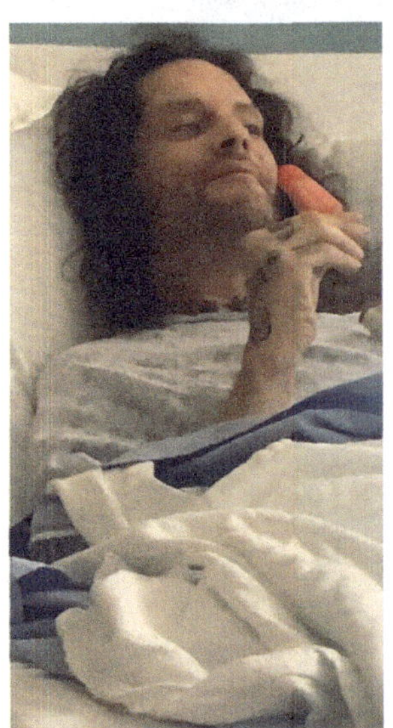

Above: On the right is a drawing I did of me and Mark together. On the left is Mark taking a selfie at home, spring 2021.

Middle: Mark enjoying one of the many popsicles he had at the Health Sciences Centre.

Bottom left: Just catching Mark off-guard again while watching a movie.

Bottom right: Mark in his dentures again. Taken in his apartment at Garrison Place.

Top: St. John's as seen from Signal Hill at night.

Middle left: Looking east down Water Street.

Middle right: Looking west down Gower Street.

Bottom: Looking east down George Street at some of the bars after a fresh snow fall. December 2020.

ACKNOWLEDGEMENTS

So aside from the obvious of Mark, who this book would never have existed without, and who I've already acknowledged in spades...I just wanted to take some time to recognize some other special people who've helped with the book or were there for Mark and me.

Firstly, I want to thank God and my Lord Jesus Christ, the rock of my salvation, for always reaching out to me even when I was not reaching for You. I can look back on all these years and see You calling me home. During all of my trials, even when I felt alone, I wasn't. You counted every tear and every heartache.

To Mom and my grandparents for raising me right and putting up with me all those years. You raised me to believe and have faith. You also dealt with many of my hardships with me as I was growing up and into adulthood. I know I could try anyone's patience. P.S. Thank you, Grandpa, for always leaving me that last piece of chocolate cake.

Jesse and Yvonne, thank you for being such wonderful friends and a part of my extended family. We've all been through so much together in a short time. I am so proud and protective of both of you, and I hope we always remain close. I hope there are many more days of hanging out and watching movies, arguing over who gets to play a song on YouTube next, and Signal Hill hikes!

My best friend, Jen, for her constant support and love. We will always have each other's back, whether in worldly issues or issues of the Spirit. To me, we are the feminine mirror of friendships like David and Jonathan in scripture. That is no small thing. Thank you for listening to me cry, laugh, and talk incessantly about the love of my life...you've been a huge support to me.

Ange, to this day, I cannot believe we ended up becoming friends. What a wonderful and unexpected gift we got. Who knew we had so much in common as we did? The Lord works in mysterious ways. He takes the bad and turns it around for good. He certainly did that in our situation. Thank you for letting me bounce ideas off you and for helping with proofreading.

James, we've spent many years sharing a love of *The Phantom of the Opera* and now here you are, all these years later, proofreading my book! You've always been a dedicated friend, and I can always count on you for a hilarious post or private message. Thanks for always being there.

Siobhan, I'm so sorry that we never got to know each other when Mark was still alive. I'm sure he gets a kick out of the fact that we are friends now. Thank you so much for sharing some things with me about Mark's childhood and various anecdotes. The funny and the serious.

Marie's Mini Mart for hiring me and letting me work for you. You gave me the opportunity to meet so many interesting people. If I hadn't been working full time at that store, I don't think I would have toughened up as much as I did professionally. Working alone in a store downtown was a lot of responsibility. If I hadn't been there, I never would have met Mark.

The nurses and staff at St. Clare's Mercy Hospital and the Health Sciences Centre in St. John's, Newfoundland, for all the hard work you put into caring for Mark. It's appreciated more than you know. I understand now just how hard nurses work. It was constant, and you are all truly angels in disguise.

I'd also like to thank anyone who let me use their real names! Ha!

Lastly, I want to thank everyone who was kind to Mark throughout his life. Thank you for seeing beneath the surface and understanding him. He was a wonderful person, and after he died, it became apparent from everyone I talked to just how many people he'd touched, even in the smallest ways. If you were a true friend to him, you are a true friend to me. Thank you.

ABOUT THE AUTHOR

Krista Cambers was born and raised in St. John's, Newfoundland, and has a deep love of her province with its rocky hills and sea air. Growing up she liked to poke around at different art forms, mostly drawing, music, and playing on her mother's typewriter.

From an early age she had the understanding that a person's position in life did not dictate their worth. This manifested itself as an adult when she fell in love with her partner Mark, a lifelong runaway. Though he is passed, she carries him with her in everything that she does. Her greatest wish is for anyone who is suffering to find love, healing, and peace in their lives and would like to do whatever she can to make the world a better place for having been here. She lives in a cozy little apartment with her cat Lumi, where she continues her artwork and hopes to write another book in the future.

CONTACT

Please feel free to contact me at:

E-Mail: LadyCambers@gmail.com

Website: http://www.markleecambers.ca

Made in the USA
Coppell, TX
02 December 2022